Praise for *Sq*

"Given the dearth of teen literature spotlighting the resistance, this work represents a valuable resource for initiates seeking firsthand information."

— *Kirkus Reviews*

"A rare, surprising tale of a teenage girl's struggle with adolescence, love of family and country, ethics, humanity, and survival under Nazi occupation of Belgium and France. That the 'Squirrel,' Mary Rostad, stayed alive as she traveled and fought against the Nazis shows the reader, young or old, what a single young person's conviction, determination, and perseverance can achieve in the name of 'Right' and justice. This is an eminently readable and inspiring book by an author who never sought the well-deserved recognition she gained late in her life. Many of the events and feelings Mary described resonate with me, a Holocaust survivor, the benefactor of the actions of a few righteous 'Squirrels.'"

—**Peter Feigl, retired
international business executive,
senior Defense Department arms negotiator,
and Holocaust lecturer and survivor**

"*Squirrel Is Alive* is a charming memoir of a young Belgian resistance fighter whose exploits during the German occupation of her country were the stuff of legend. As a young woman, she served as a courier transferring information, arms, and ammunition between resistance groups defying the Nazis and leading a daring and adventurous life. Her journey took her into the arms of a liberating American soldier and into small-town America where she worked as a nurse and then, later in life, where she spoke to groups large and small about her experience and the meaning of freedom and democracy, values that Americans too easily take for granted. It brought her well-deserved honors, but more importantly, brought wisdom and insight to her many audiences. The issues she spoke of, the questions she raised, and the values she embodied have become more urgent in our world, and Squirrel—her code name during the war—is once again alive through this moving memoir, alive with much to say."

— **Michael Berenbaum,**
Distinguished Professor of Jewish Studies and
Director, Sigi Ziering Holocaust Institute

"A teenager makes a difference. Mary Rostad sees her country is being destroyed by the Nazis, so the 'Squirrel,' as she is known, leaves her family and walks over a thousand miles in the cold with little food, always in constant danger, to report German troop movements. She was not a bystander but an upstander, a hero. At the end of the war, she visits Dachau and learns that President Eisenhower insisted the townspeople see the atrocities caused by the Nazis, an action that could have predicted the eventual rise of Holocaust deniers. Toward the end of her life, Mary—with the encouragement of her mentor, Darryle Clott—feels compelled to share her experiences with the world."

—Sam Harris, President Emeritus and founding member, Illinois Holocaust Museum; Holocaust survivor

"Relatable stories of heroism can be transformative because they remind us of our values, fears, love, and humanity. This is the story of Mary Rostad, a typical teenage schoolgirl who in 1940 rebelled against the Nazi occupation of her homeland in Brussels. Her defiance began with small acts of sabotage and rose to organized resistance. At the age of seventeen, Mary, code name "Squirrel," left home with nothing but the clothes on her back, braided ponytails, and her teenage heart fueled by a rebellious spirit grounded in the value of justice. She spent two years evading Nazi capture as a courier for the resistance. Risking her life for justice, freedom, and democracy, Mary reminds us of the courage our inner voice carries and the power of our youth. Our students need such stories."

—**Lesly Culp**
USC Shoah Foundation
Director of Education and Outreach

SQUIRREL IS ALIVE

The Servant Leadership Series

Series Editor: Dr. Richard Kyte, Director of the
D.B. Reinhart Institute for Ethics in Leadership and
Endowed Professor of Ethics at Viterbo University

What Is Servant Leadership?

Servant leadership stems from the conviction that the best leaders are those who have a deep personal commitment to the common good—that is, to the well-being of all and not just a few—and out of that commitment comes the desire to lead. What this means is that good leadership cannot be defined merely in terms of principles, techniques, or strategies; it is primarily a matter of character, originating in love and culminating in effective action. The foundational insight of servant leadership is that all leadership, properly understood, is an exercise of virtue and can be evaluated according to whether it leads to a flourishing life for individuals and communities. The practice of servant leadership seeks to inspire and engage people to work for the greater good every day.

The D.B Reinhart Institute for Ethics in Leadership

Since 1999, the D.B. Reinhart Institute for Ethics in Leadership at Viterbo University has brought people together in fruitful conversation about ethical ideas and issues, inspiring people to lead ethical lives while at the same time helping to develop leadership abilities to further the common good in communities and organizations.

**An online study guide for *Squirrel Is Alive*
is available at
https://www.viterbo.edu/db-reinhart-institute-
ethics-leadership/teaching-holocaust-workshop**

SQUIRREL IS ALIVE

A Teenager in the Belgian Resistance and French Underground

Mary Rostad

with Susan T. Hessel

Revised and Edited by
Stephen Feinberg

Fulcrum Publishing
Wheat Ridge, Colorado

Originally published in 2012 by the D.B. Reinhart Institute for
Ethics in Leadership at Viterbo University

Library of Congress Cataloging-in-Publication Data

Names: Rostad, Mary, 1924-2011 author. | Hessel, Susan T., author.
Title: Squirrel is alive : a teenager in the Belgian Resistance and French under-
  ground / Mary Rostad, with Susan T. Hessel.
Other titles: Teenager in the Belgian Resistance and French underground
Description: Wheat Ridge, Colorado : Fulcrum Publishing, 2023. | Series: The
  Servant Leadership Series | "Originally published in 2012 by the D.B. Reinhart
  Institute for Ethics in Leadership at Viterbo University."--Tile page verso.
Identifiers: LCCN 2022053102 (print) | LCCN 2022053103 (ebook) | ISBN
  9781682753774 (paperback) | ISBN 9781682753781 (ebook)
Subjects: LCSH: Rostad, Mary, 1924-2011--Childhood and youth. |
  Belgium--History--German occupation, 1940-1945. | World War,
  1939-1945--Underground movements--Belgium. | World War,
  1939-1945--Underground movements--France. | World War,
  1939-1945--Personal narratives, Belgian. | BISAC: HISTORY / Wars & Con-
  flicts / World War II / General
Classification: LCC D802.B4 R67 2023 (print) | LCC D802.B4 (ebook) | DDC
  940.53493092 [B]--dc23/eng/20230112
LC record available at https://lccn.loc.gov/2022053102
LC ebook record available at https://lccn.loc.gov/2022053103

Printed in the United States
0 9 8 7 6 5 4 3 2 1

Photos of Mary Rostad courtesy of her children,
Andre, Denise, and Kim Rostad
Photo of USA Today newspaper clipping © USA TODAY NETWORK
Photo of Elie Wiesel, Mary Rostad, and Darryle Clott
courtesy of David Joseph Marcou

Cover design by Kateri Kramer
Cover images courtesy of Andre, Denise, and Kim Rostad

Fulcrum Publishing
3970 Youngfield Street • Wheat Ridge, Colorado 80033
(800) 992-2908 • (303) 277-1623 • www.fulcrumbooks.com

CONTENTS

FOREWORD

BY ALEXANDRA ZAPRUDER

One early morning in March 1942, a teenage girl walked away from her life, her parents, and her home to join the fight against fascism. Without saying goodbye to her beloved parents, she set out to walk more than 1,100 miles from her home in Brussels through France, Spain, and into Portugal, where she hoped a ship would take her to England to join the Free Belgian forces fighting the Germans. "My plans," she admitted, "were big and bold— incredibly naive!" Nothing could have prepared her for the fear, loneliness, and physical endurance that lay ahead.

In this memoir, Mary Rostad tells her story as a member of the Belgian resistance—code name Squirrel— with disarming candor, recalling frankly that at least some of it was an adventure undertaken by an impulsive teen with "more guts than brains." At the same time, she captures vividly her own and her fellow Belgians' deep resentment of the German presence, which motivated the entire nation to mobilize in whatever way they could against the aggressor. On the individual level, Mary reflects on her family's history—her grandfather's use of carrier pigeons to secretly send messages to the Allies in World War I and her mother's resourcefulness in providing for her family during the occupation—which taught her that the response to injustice was not to be a victim but to take action.

Immediately following the occupation, Mary worked with the Girl Scouts to offer rolls and coffee to departing troops and took medic classes to prepare to care for the wounded, which would bring her face-to-face with gruesome violence for the first time. When she and her friends were conscripted to work in a German flashlight factory, they found ways to sabotage the work. From there, she explains, she was gradually drawn into the work, distributing leaflets, passing small arms and messages to the underground, and pouring sugar into German gas tanks and slashing their tires.

But it was the decision to leave home, her long journey across Europe reporting German troop movement to the underground through regular meetings with unnamed contacts, that forms the heart of this story. Far from presenting herself as a hero, Mary tells her own story with honesty, humor, and perspective. At the same time, she reminds us that it was precisely her identity as a teen girl that provided the cover for her activities. Since no one took her particularly seriously, or even noticed her with her small stature and pigtails, nobody suspected the depths of her courage and the risks she was willing to take.

For millions of young readers everywhere, it is Anne Frank's voice and words that epitomize the experience of young people during the Holocaust and World War II. Anne's diary reveals an equally plucky and vibrant young soul, one who had to hide away in order to try to survive. But unlike Anne Frank, Mary Rostad could have stayed at home. She could have stayed out of trouble. She was not Jewish; she was not in any way a particular target of the Germans. She could have waited it out and let others do the heavy lifting of resistance.

But she didn't. By her own admission, through a combination of national pride, teenage rebelliousness, and youthful naivete, she responded to her own conscience and stepped into action. She did not wait for someone else to save her and her family; she took it upon herself to do what she could with the tools at her disposal. Writing from the vantage point of many years after the war, it's easy to forget that she risked her life for the principles of justice, freedom, and democracy. But that is exactly what she did.

We have plenty of examples of adults who took these risks. But while many young people across Europe participated in the underground, few people know their names or remember them. The cumulative effect of this is to forget the way that young people can and did draw upon the very particular gifts of adolescence to do their part to restore order to a broken and violated world.

In this story of courage, resilience, youthful idealism, and national pride, Mary Rostad reminds young readers everywhere that the power to act is in our own hands, even in the smallest ways. She reminds us to honor the quiet voice inside that refuses to accept injustice and that finds its own ways to resist. It is a story, in the end, of an ordinary girl with an ordinary life who did something extraordinary when the circumstances called for it. Her name and her story deserve to be remembered for what she did so many decades ago and for what she can inspire us to do today.

INTRODUCTION
MY JOURNEY BEGINS

After weeks and maybe months on the road from Brussels, Belgium, to what I hoped would eventually mean joining the Free Belgian forces in England, I was more than ready to rest. I was passed from contact to contact in the Belgian Resistance and later the French Underground during World War II.

If lucky, I slept at night in a church or railroad sidecar. If I was not so lucky, I camped in a barn. I always hated that because I am deathly afraid of mice. My only clothes were the ones I wore when I left home.

I had little to eat those weeks, mainly just a few carrots or apples I found along the road. A rare piece of bread was a feast if I was lucky enough to find a family willing to give me this treat. Eating one apple is a good thing, but when it is your steady diet with little else it does nasty things to your insides, something so hard to deal with on the road.

Being nearly eighteen with my hair in pigtails, I looked young and innocent. That made it easier—but no safer—to pass messages, small arms, and sometimes ammunition to freedom fighters.

Looking back, I can't believe what I put my parents through during the two years I lived under the Nazis in

Belgium and my two years on the road. I did not even say goodbye to my parents that morning I left, other than to pretend I was off to work for the hated Nazis in a factory.

I started walking with little money, no food, and no change of clothes. All I had was a summer coat, certainly not one that would get me through the winter, but then I didn't expect to be on the road for so long.

I chose not to carry the all-important identification papers, even though I knew I would have to produce them at the whim of any German demanding them. In Europe during those awful days, papers were everything, especially to the Germans who kept meticulous records of every person in every country they occupied.

Why did I not carry these papers? I knew being found with them would put my parents back home at greater risk as the Germans believed in "collective responsibility." I had heard too many stories of the Nazis torturing and killing an entire family when a loved one was captured while helping the underground. Without the papers identifying me, only I was at risk of being imprisoned, tortured, and shot—not my parents, brother, and sisters.

So I left home and kept on walking one March morning in 1942. I had just a vague notion of where I would meet my first contact in Waterloo, that place in Belgium where Napoleon suffered his final military loss nearly 130 years earlier. I was to meet this unnamed person at La Butte du Lion, "statue of a lion." That statue of a lion was located on a hill that looked toward France as a reminder to the French of their loss to the nations aligned against Napoleon in that long-ago battle.

As instructed, I sat at the bottom of the hill and waited—but not too long. Soon a man came and planted himself next to me. I knew he was my connection when he said, "I come every day to feed the squirrels."

My code name, Squirrel, came from my nickname in Girl Scouts. We used code names for each other in the resistance because it was too dangerous to know each other's real identities.

This man stopped only long enough to tell me where I was to go next. And so it went, day after day, week after week, and month after month.

It was all so foolish and yet so important; it was an adventure and youthful silliness and very serious business. I felt I had to do this. I was not the only teenager to be so bold in those days. I was among hundreds and maybe thousands of young people who left home to fight back against the German invasion of our country in any way we could.

I was exhausted, hungry, and cold much of the time as I weaved back and forth between contacts across France. After so much time without rest, I looked forward to being in what was called a safe house—a place where resistance workers on the run could stay without fear and (we hoped) without detection. When one such place was described to me, I imagined the opportunity to take a bath and wash my clothes. I dreamed of a good meal for once. Yes, I would connect with people who felt the same way I did about the Nazi invasion and occupation of Belgium and France.

But just as I turned the corner into the block where the safe house was located in Lyon, France, I heard a sound that was as terrifying as it got in those days—the wails of a siren. With heart-pounding fear, I quietly turned back and quickly—but calmly—walked away.

Had I arrived five minutes earlier at the safe house I would have been in the hands of the Gestapo. You would not be reading this book.

CHAPTER ONE

MY COUNTRY INVADED

It is hard for Americans—whose country has never been occupied by another nation other than the British during the American Revolution—to understand just what it meant to us when Germany invaded Belgium on May 10, 1940. I was scared, frustrated, and angry. As a teenager with more guts than brains, I naturally wanted to fight back any time I was told I could not do something. And that happened constantly under the Germans.

By 1938, two years before the bombs fell on Brussels, where I was born, we knew Germany had an aggressive foreign policy. Belgians feared what was ahead for our own little country. King Leopold III had expressly said Belgium would remain neutral in the event of war: "We should remain resolute at placing us outside any dispute of our neighbors."[1]

Many people believed in the early 1930s that Adolf Hitler was a desperate and funny little man who could never gain the kind of power that led his nation into World War II. Surely, the German people would never take him seriously; they would see him as the madman he was.

Many also thought the Treaty of Versailles, signed after World War I, would protect the world from another war with Germany. It forced Germany to disarm, greatly reduce its military and air force, and to pay reparations.

As the US Holocaust Memorial Museum explains,

> Perhaps the most humiliating portion of the treaty for defeated Germany was Article 231, commonly known as the 'War Guilt Clause,' which forced the German nation to accept complete responsibility for initiating World War I. As such Germany was liable for all material damages, and France's premier, Georges Clemenceau, particularly insisted on imposing enormous reparation payments. Aware that Germany would probably not be able to pay such a towering debt, Clemenceau and the French nevertheless greatly feared rapid German recovery and the initiation of a new war against France. Hence, the French sought in the postwar treaty to limit Germany's potential to regain its economic superiority and to rearm.[2]

Between hyperinflation of the German currency, the Great Depression, and huge war reparations, the German economy was destabilized, with unemployment nearly tripling in 1931, rising from 1.5 million to 4.3 million with massive poverty and starvation. By 1932, unemployment reached 6 million.

Adolf Hitler, who had once been tried for treason, became a kind of savior to the German people—who cheered when he was appointed chancellor on January 30, 1933. Four weeks later, the German Parliament (the Reichstag) was set aflame, which led to the government suspending civil rights and the creation of a state of emergency.

Hitler used propaganda techniques from World War I that he and his Nazi party literally turned into an art form—to convince the German people he was the answer to all their problems. After German president Paul von Hindenburg died in 1934, Hitler became president as well as chancellor. Everyone was to swear personal allegiance to him as the Führer, who was above all laws.[3]

Hitler's rise of power also appealed to those who felt German honor had been lost in the wake of the Treaty of Versailles. In hours-long speeches in mass rallies, Hitler promised to return Germany to its former glory. To do that, Hitler chose a scapegoat—Jews, whom he villainized along with Communists and Socialists.

Also under Hitler, Germany ignored the Treaty of Versailles and built up its powerful military force. In the late 1930s, Germany invaded or took over other countries, including Austria and Czechoslovakia. By 1935, the German military draft was reinstituted and the Wehrmacht—the Germany Army—grew to 550,000 men—all in violation of the Versailles treaty.

Hitler remilitarized the Rhineland on March 7, 1936, again in violation of the Treaty of Versailles. When Britain and France only condemned the action but did not take action against him, Hitler was emboldened. Those countries were so war-weary and struggling economically in their own depressions that they did not want to get into another conflict. They tried treaties of their own to prevent wars. Hitler only saw weakness in Britain and France.

The Nazis took over Austria in March 1938, making it part of Germany—a union called the Anschluss. In September 1938, the Sudetenland, an area of Czechoslovakia with a German ethnic majority, was handed over to Germany in order to avoid a new European war. Then, in March 1939, the Germans took over the remaining parts of Czechoslovakia.

When Germany and Russia signed a nonaggression pact in August 1939, many were startled as no one thought they would join together. Germany invaded Poland on September 1, 1939, but split the occupation of that country with Russia.

Great Britain and France, having given guarantees to Poland that they would declare war on Germany if Polish independence came under threat, entered the war on September 3, 1939. When Germany invaded Poland, they had no choice but to go to war.

Even after Hitler's army invaded Belgium and France on May 10, 1940, he was not satisfied. In June 1941, Germany ignored its alliance with the Soviet Union, took over the parts of Poland under Soviet control, and attacked Russia directly.

Meanwhile, many in the United States were trying to remain neutral—isolated from the war in Europe. President Franklin Roosevelt was alarmed by events in Europe. He proposed the United States manufacture and send aircraft, tanks, ships, trucks, munitions, food, and services to fight Germany through the Lend-Lease Program. Ostensibly, the $50 billion in ships, equipment, and ammunitions that went to Britain, France, and China would be paid for and then returned when the war was over. The program, formally known as an Act to Further Promote the Defense of the United States, helped to get the nation into war production before it was attacked at Pearl Harbor on December 7, 1941.

As a family and in school, we followed Hitler's invasion of countries across Europe in newspapers, radio, and newsreels at the movies. You did not have to speak German to recognize how hypnotic his voice was when he ranted for hours in speeches to tens of thousands of his people in public squares. He captivated his audience, which responded with a passion I have not seen since. The German people appeared ready to do anything their Führer (German for absolute leader) ordered, including killing millions of innocents or even each other at his command.

Throughout history, my little country always found itself in the path of conquering nations. To our north is the Netherlands, to our south is France, to the west is the North Sea, across which is Great Britain. Most significant, to the east is the even smaller Luxembourg and more ominously, Germany. Historically, we spoke Dutch in Belgium because we were once part of Holland. But in the nineteenth and twentieth centuries, French became the common language, although some Belgians still spoke Flemish, which is similar to Dutch.

Brussels—the capital and largest city—was called a "fortress city" as early as the tenth century. After walls were built around the city in the thirteenth century, this capital area of Belgium grew rapidly. A second tier of walls was constructed in the fourteenth century.

French artillery bombarded the city in 1695, destroying 4,000 buildings, about a third of the city. The French captured Brussels in 1746 in the War of Austrian Succession. Three years later, Belgium was turned over to the Austrians.

In 1815, Napoleon Bonaparte lost his last battle—the Battle of Waterloo—in what is today part of Belgium but was then in the United Kingdom of the Netherlands. The battlefield is eight miles southeast of Brussels, about a mile from the town of Waterloo. That battle meant the end of Napoleon's rule as emperor of France.

Belgium never wanted to be at war, always preferring the sidelines. It declared its neutrality when hostilities broke out in both World War I and World War II. Our attempts at neutrality did us no good—Germany invaded us in both wars.

Belgium in World War I

In writing *Belgium Unvanquished*, which told the story of Belgium during World War II, author Roger Motz described the important impact the First World War had on my country. At the time of World War I, Belgium was the most population-dense country in the world and one that had a very strong economy and the world's wealthiest city in Antwerp, the port city. The German invasion of Belgium in 1914 and four years of occupation "put an end to this long period of economic prosperity and social progress,"[4] Motz wrote in the midst of the Second World War in 1942.

In addition to the destruction of many towns and villages, women and children were massacred. The Germans also caused tremendous inflation during the occupation by devaluing the Belgium currency. The price of the human misery cannot be calculated.

As Motz wrote about Belgium during World War I,

> The Germans were faced with the patriotic resistance of the population. . . . In spite of the ever-increasing arrests, in spite of fines imposed on towns and communes, Belgian citizens never failed to reveal their feelings. Just as in this war [World War II], the Belgians were the first to adopt the "V" as a sign of their confidence in Victory, so during the years 1914–18, they wore in their buttonholes ivy leaves as a sign of hope and of their attachment to their invaded Fatherland.[5]

World War I was a very brutal war because of a madness called trench warfare. For months on end, each side dug trenches, shooting periodically at the other side across a barbed wire divide. In Belgium alone, some 58,637 people died in combat along with 62,000 civilians.

You may have heard the poem and song, "In Flanders Field," which was written in 1915 in response to so many lives lost in Flanders, an area in northern Belgium that is the home of the Flemish people. Today portions of Flanders Fields are in Belgium, France, and Holland.

The poem and later a song with the same words memorialized the horrific loss of life during any war. It referred specifically to the World War I Battles of Ypres, during which tens of thousands of men died. Lieutenant Colonel John McCrae, a doctor serving in the Canadian Army, wrote the poem after observing how many poppies had sprung up on the sacred land where so many fell and were buried.

> *In Flanders fields the poppies blow*
> *Between the crosses row on row,*
> *That mark our place; and in the sky*
> *The larks, still bravely singing, fly*
> *Scarce heard amid the guns below.*
>
> *We are the Dead. Short days ago*
> *We lived, felt dawn, saw sunset glow,*
> *Loved and were loved, and now we lie*
> *In Flanders fields.*
>
> *Take up our quarrel with the foe:*
> *To you from failing hands we throw*
> *The torch; be yours to hold it high.*
> *If ye break faith with us who die*
> *We shall not sleep, though poppies grow*
> *In Flanders fields.*

Three Belgian leaders—King Albert I, Cardinal Désiré-Félicien-François-Joseph Mercier, and Burgomaster Adolphe Max—led resistance in the country during the four years of occupation beginning in 1914. When the Germans demanded passage through Belgium to France, King

Albert said, "I rule a nation, not a road." The king took command of the Belgian Army, fighting with it while his wife, the queen, worked at the front as a nurse. Their son, Prince Leopold, at age twelve, enlisted in the Belgian Army.

Cardinal Mercier wrote a pastoral letter, "Patriotism and Endurance," which was read in churches across the country, leading to the deaths of thirteen priests and arrests of many more by the occupying Germans. The cardinal was held under house arrest. Max, mayor of Brussels, refused to collaborate with the Germans. That led to the mayor's arrest.

Meanwhile, General Moritz von Bissing, the governor-general of occupied Belgium, was said to be "a hard and unscrupulous man and well-versed in duplicity. In order to quell the resistance of the people, he set out to split Belgium by provoking hostility between the Flemings and Walloons."[6] He actually separated Belgium into two regions—Flanders and Wallonia.

The Walloons and Flemings still are the two main ethnic groups in Belgium. The Walloons—found mostly in southern provinces—speak French, while the Flemings speak Flemish, a language similar to Dutch. The Flemings, who were considered Germanic during World War I, historically lived in northern Belgium.

French became the official language of Belgium after the country separated from the Netherlands in 1830. The Flemish later were associated with rural poverty and a lack of education. During World War I, the language difference meant the Belgian officers who spoke French could not speak with Flemish-speaking troops.[7]

Belgium was in terrible shape after World War I, like the rest of the world. In *Belgium: A History*, author Bernard A. Cook described the country as being in a "sorry state." "Of all the participants in World War I, Belgium, which had not wished to be part of the struggle, suffered proportionately the greatest physical destruction."[8]

He noted that more than 100,000 homes were destroyed, as were 300,000 acres of farmland. Rail lines and locomotives, and forty-six of the nation's fifty-one steel mills were either destroyed or damaged. He put the value of the loss in 1918 dollars at $7 billion, which would be equal to about $99 billion today. Cook noted Belgium somehow had rebuilt its damaged cities by the mid-1920s.

CHAPTER TWO

MY FAMILY

I was born on September 19, 1924. I had a pretty normal childhood for the times, which were not that easy with so much unemployment during the Great Depression of the 1930s. My parents, Maurice and Mathilde Brouillard, always found a way to put food on the table for our family of eight, which included my paternal grandmother and the five children: Andre, Marguerite (Maggy, known as Daisy), Angele, Renee, and me.

My father, who served in the Belgian Army for two years after World War I, was a civil engineer who worked for a company that went bankrupt during the Great Depression. We lived in a building that housed a café that my father ran in Buizingen, a village in the municipality of Halle, Belgium, nine miles southwest of the center of Brussels.

This building was large—bigger than the town hall in the city of Houston, Minnesota, where I now live. It was truly a community center with six pool tables and an upstairs dance hall and theater stage. Anyone who wanted to dance could feed the jukebox. Sometimes movies were shown there or sewing machines were demonstrated. Outside, there were games, including handball.

My father sold the café and building to Uncle Louis and Aunt Anna, who, as my mother's oldest sister, was my godmother. My dad then bought a grocery store in Brussels, but that business didn't work out. Papa was most successful as a maître d' and head waiter at Cap du Nord in Brussels, a busy family restaurant close to the railroad station in the middle of town.

We lived in a not-so-nice apartment for about two or three years before moving into a house in the Brussels suburb of Forest, which was considered to be an "ideal" community. The houses, whether rented or owned, were designed for families with children with their front and back gardens. Parents felt comfortable with their children out playing anywhere in the neighborhood.

My mother, Mathilde Crab Brouillard, was born in Uccle, Belgium, about four miles southwest of Brussels, to François and Augustine Crab. Her mother died suddenly one night at the dinner table of a cerebral hemorrhage (bleeding in the tissues in the brain, a leading cause of stroke). That death must have been absolutely terrifying to Maman, who had not yet married my father.

My parents never talked with us about their experiences during World War I. However, by 1939, they began to worry about what the Nazis were doing elsewhere in Europe. My mother then would describe life in a country at war, particularly one occupied by the Germans. She didn't tell me those stories to scare me, but to prepare me for hard times ahead.

As Roger Motz wrote, "Belgians remembered the German occupation [in World War I] as the most fearful, the most cruel experience. Moreover, their country had been ruined in spite of the Allied victory. . . . Belgians had a more realistic and more precise idea of what a German occupation was really like—poverty, famine, humiliations, the constant threat of arrest."[9]

Being naive and idealistic, I heard the stories of danger and thought how exciting it must have been to live through that war or any war. But then, I had only seen war in the movies. We all loved movies, which we went to any chance we had. Often those movies came from America and included Westerns with cowboy singer Gene Autry. I always rooted for the Indians, although I'm not sure why, other than they were the underdogs.

I could never understand racism. We had people with darker skin color in Belgium in part because of the Belgian Congo, just one of many European colonies that amassed wealth from the vast minerals found there for its ruling countries. The Congo, under the direct control of King Leopold II, was the site of horrific genocide and civil war before it became an independent nation in 1960. Sadly, it has been unstable for many years since.

In Brussels, we might not like someone on a personal level who was of a different race, but it was not because we viewed them racially. We didn't care if people were black, white, or purple. I thought someone like my classmate Bombula, who gained that unusual name because her father had been stationed in Africa, was exotic and exciting. Just living somewhere else seemed thrilling to me.

I was soon to learn attitudes in Germany were even worse toward minority groups, something that my parents had experienced and observed in the First World War.

My parents told me about the role of Grandfather François Crab during World War I. He courageously used his carrier pigeons to send messages to the Allies from occupied Belgium. Long since replaced by communications technology, even having them was grounds for execution if caught. Maman told me how frightening it was when Germans broke into their home searching for evidence of collaboration with the Allies. Thankfully, they never found any.

Grandfather's actions made a big impression on me—I was not quite sixteen years old when the Germans invaded. I didn't think then of the terrible things that happen in war. Instead, I had these grandiose ideas about heroism and actions I would take against an oppressor.

Like the United States and the rest of Europe, Belgium struggled during the Great Depression, with unprecedented unemployment. Jobs that were available were low paying. The economy was so unstable that Belgium had four different governments in one two-year period. With such conditions across Europe in the 1930s, the stage was set for people to embrace fanaticism and demagoguery.

My Childhood

When we lived in Forest, I walked the five blocks to the Catholic elementary school for two years and later fifteen blocks to another school, coming home for lunch through seventh grade.

For about three or four years, I attended the Lycée, which is a secondary school between elementary school and university.

I remember an outbreak of diphtheria when I was a small child. Maman took me with her when she cared for the neighbors' children. Since they were kept in isolation, I must already have had the illness, or she could not have taken me with her. Maman was there because the little ones' mothers were too scared to follow the prescribed treatment.

I can still hear and see these little children cry when Maman scrubbed their throats with a long round brush dipped in methylene blue to safely break the membranes that closed their airways. I heard a doctor tell my mother that she had saved many lives by doing that. From that moment on, I wanted to be a doctor. The German invasion of Belgium in May 1940 changed those plans.

Another of my earliest memories, when I was about eight years old, involved walking to St. Denis Church for Sunday mass with my friend Louisette, and a couple other girls. My parents did not attend church often, but one or the other usually walked with us to the door. On this day, we were allowed to make the short walk to church on our own. In our purses were coins we were supposed to deposit in the collection box.

The church was near a shopping area, Place St. Denis, in Forest, not far from our home. We looked in different shop windows on the way, including an ice cream parlor that listed all sorts of delightful concoctions on its sign. Prices appeared so reasonable that we felt we could afford a treat with those cents in our purses—if we did not give them to the church. No one would have to know, and next week we would make up for it.

Mireille (Mary) with her parents, Mathilde and Maurice Brouillard. The matting behind the photo is a letter Maurice wrote Mathilde when they were engaged.

Mary (left) in the early 1930s with her brother, Andre; father, Maurice; and mother, Mathilde, who has Maggy in her arms.

I ordered a "White Lady," a wonderful sundae with mounds of vanilla ice cream covered with chocolate and cherries on top. I can still taste that delicious treat. When the waiter came with our bill, we nearly fell over. "It can't be right," I said. "The sign says thirty-five centime."

Boy, did he laugh. We owed about ten times what was on an old sign. It had been there for something like twenty or thirty years. That old sign was similar to the old advertising signs that decorate shops today in the United States, as a relic of an earlier time.

I called Papa, who unhappily came to our rescue. He didn't get upset often, but this time he was quite angry with me, although he did not spank me. Not only was it wrong to not give the church the money, I had gone into that shop without enough money to pay for the ice cream. I certainly heard about what I had done. It was quite a while before I had the nerve to walk into any shop without Papa or Maman, who carried the money.

Our kitchen was the heart of our old brick home on the Avenue de Fleron in Forest. Our house was like many homes on this tree-lined street, all with gardens full of flowers and lawns with neat little edges.

We had a large oak table inlaid with ceramic, an old green sideboard, and Grandmother Brouillard's old cookstove. This coal stove was a thing of beauty with the front and sides covered with green tiles painted with white daisies. It also was our family room, where we ate our meals, did our homework, and played games. From the large kitchen window, Maman kept an eye on the children playing in the backyard with its large cherry tree.

Our home was a meeting place for our friends and neighbors. It felt normal then, but now I know that my parents were unusual. Their coffeepot was always on the stove, and women often came to my mother for advice about their children's health. The men asked my father about their legal problems and businesses. They just knew that Mathilde and Maurice would listen to them and answer their questions.

Sometimes when I smell toast, I think of the grilled toast that Bobonne (my grandmother) used to make. She shined the top of the stove with wax paper and then placed slices of bread right on it. It tasted so good with fresh butter and a sprinkle of brown sugar.

I remember a time in grade school when I was jealous that a classmate had broken an arm or leg. It seemed so glamorous that everyone wanted to help her that I secretly wished I were the one with the broken bone.

A few years later my friends and I were coming home from school, crowding the sidewalk. I don't remember what I said in my conversation with my friend Armand, but he responded, "I don't believe it!" and poked me on the shoulder. It was light, but just enough for me to lose my balance and go sprawling into the middle of the street.

A car driver slammed on his brakes to stop—and did so right on my knees. He backed off as my friends were screaming. Luckily, it happened right in front of a doctor's office.

"Don't move!" my friends yelled.

Embarrassed and with my usual determination, I got right up to walk to the doctor's office myself, only to fall right back down. I fainted.

They must have carried me into the doctor's house. After an examination, he identified ruptured bursa in both knees. The bursa is a sack of fluid that acts as a cushion between bones and the muscles around a joint. My friends carried me home with strict orders to keep both my legs elevated. I stayed home from school for two weeks with medications to keep me comfortable. Maman and Papa put a lounge chair in the backyard so I could lie under a cherry tree to read.

A police officer came by to learn more about the injury. They wanted to know if it had been intentional. I told the officer that it was just an accident. I didn't want anyone to get in trouble because of my own foolishness.

It was a wonderful vacation with neighbors and friends stopping by with gifts—fruit, cakes, and flowers. Every day was like Christmas, and I was like a princess receiving offers from her loyal subjects. Even the weather was unusual—the sun shone every day for two weeks, something that was very unusual for Brussels. Maman brought me meals on trays and friends entertained me. What a vacation! If this was suffering, I loved every minute of it—even if I did not get a cast out of it.

My Best Friend—Aunt Juliette

After Grandmother Crab died, her youngest daughter, Aunt Juliette, went to live with Aunt Angele and Uncle Henry, who did not have children of their own. I remember her as beautiful with auburn hair and being very smart.

Whenever we made our frequent trips to visit Aunt Angele, I slept with Aunt Juliette, who told the four- or five-year-old me about her boyfriends and the fun things she did. She didn't find me to be a pesky little kid like most teenagers did. Instead, she taught me how to dance the Charleston, which was very popular then.

One time she took me with her to visit a friend who lived on a farm. Her friend's father showed me all sorts of things, including how to make a playhouse out of bunches of straw and how to slip my hand delicately under hens to gather their eggs. He taught me how to remove a raw egg without breaking the shell. He had me make a little hole on each side, take a breath, and suck out the egg, which I swallowed. Now, of course, it would be very dangerous to eat a raw egg in that way because of concerns about salmonella or another form of food poisoning. Maybe my mother knew even then it was not a good idea because when I told her, she almost fainted.

That Sunday morning Aunt Juliette dressed me for church in a white organdy dress with pink smocking that she had made for me. I wore pretty white leggings and Mary Jane shoes. She spent much time brushing my hair until it just shone. Then, still needing to get dressed herself, she sent me outside with reminders not to get dirty.

Young Mary and her aunt Juliette shopping in Brussels.

Seeing a mound of dirt in the backyard, I decided to jump over it, convinced I would easily sail across this mound left by a cow. Imagine what it did to my Sunday best. Needless to say, we didn't go to church that Sunday, and it was a long time before Aunt Juliette took me with her again.

She did not a hold a grudge, though. When her boyfriends came they always talked with me. One even took me on a long, fast motorcycle ride. It was a thrill for a little girl. We went so fast my hair flew.

I loved watching Aunt Juliette get ready to go dancing. She was my idol, wearing the nicest clothes, like a pale blue flowing dress edged with marabou (stork-like) feathers. She twirled for me in the living room, and then she took my hands and we waltzed until we were both dizzy.

Aunt Juliette, who never finished high school, had such nerve. When she applied for a job and her prospective boss asked if she could type, she said of course she could. When the boss asked her to demonstrate for him, she said, "This is not the keyboard I am used to. It will take me a little while."

The truth is she had never typed a single letter in her life. She was hired and worked for that company for two years, including serving as the boss's private secretary. She later purchased her own specialty cheese shop on a street in Brussels known for premier shops. She handled her place with such grace and sometimes took me with her to work, where she introduced me to her customers.

It soon changed when Fernand arrived on the scene. He appeared charming and always brought Aunt Juliette fresh flowers and candy, but I didn't like him from the beginning. He was so different from her other boyfriends, and he took her away from me.

I was a flower girl at their magnificent wedding, which had all the trappings of a royal wedding—limousines, the church decorations, the reception, and the flowers. In my young eyes, it seemed like the kind of wedding a princess would have.

I still went to visit my aunt after the wedding, but it was never the same again. Fernand had changed dramatically after he came home from Germany where he was held as a World War I prisoner. He became a religious fanatic who opposed many things Aunt Juliette enjoyed. He would not allow my aunt to sing around the house, and he burned all the sheet music of songs she loved.

Aunt Juliette and Uncle Fernand had five children, whom she cared for without her husband providing much financial support. Despite their living in poverty, Fernand would not allow anyone from her family to help them.

Sadly, Aunt Juliette developed breast cancer in 1950, which she fought with many trips to the hospital. The nurses called her their "sun ray," as she could always bolster the other patients' spirits. She never complained. She was such a giver. For me she was more than a friend; she was willing to share her joy with me when I was a little girl.

I still think of my aunt, who was my best friend as a little girl, whenever I see the touch of auburn in my daughter Denise's hair or in my granddaughter Aimee.

Great-Aunt Philomene and Grandfather Crab

Visiting Philomene, my dad's aunt and my great-aunt, was always fun because she had many stories to tell and didn't mind little girls playing with her treasures. I remember the colorful geraniums on each step going up to her second-floor apartment in a large brownstone. Her salon, or living room as we call it today, was filled with Victorian furniture. We always heard Enrico Caruso's voice on her large gramophone—the first device that allowed us to listen to recorded music. Caruso, an Italian tenor, was among the first to make recordings—290—between 1902 and 1920.

What I remember most was taking my favorite doll to visit her. Without fail, she got out her sewing basket with silks and laces and made my baby the most beautiful clothes. Her stitches were so small and even, and her designs elegant. Of course, she did have a son who worked for the Singer Sewing Machine Company as regional director in the Belgian Congo.

My *grand-père* (grandfather) Crab was my mother's father. I remember him being cantankerous because he was in ill health. During most of the years that my parents took care of him, he was bedridden. He got help—or our attention—by hitting his cane against the wall. I remember how he shook that cane to scare me. It worked.

Grandfather liked to embarrass everyone around him, including a school friend of his who was a very dignified clergyman. Grandfather ordinarily didn't swear—except when this friend visited. Then he was in rare form, using words we had never heard around the house otherwise—words that made Maman blush.

As a young man, Grandfather supported his wife and three children without a job other than teaching swimming. After finding a bank bag full of money, he did the right thing instead of keeping the money for himself. The surprised bank officer responded to his honesty by offering Grandfather a job. This was the same principled grandfather who used his pigeons to transport messages to the Allies.

New Year's Day 1930—The Funeral

It was the practice on New Year's Day to visit relatives to offer good wishes for the year. In 1930, when I was just six, I was dressed in my white bunny-fur coat to go visiting with Papa and Grandfather Emile Brouillard. Maman had to stay home because three-year-old Andre and my infant sister Daisy had the measles.

When we arrived with our gaily wrapped candy, my great-aunt opened the door in tears. I climbed the stairs to the second floor, hanging on to Papa's hand tightly because I knew something was wrong.

A man was on each side of my great-uncle—Grandfather's brother. They were pumping his arms up and down—some sort of cardiopulmonary resuscitation used in those days. To me, he just looked pale. Realizing how serious the situation was, I was sent downstairs to look at the birds in a large gold cage in the living room.

After what seemed like a very long time, Papa came down with my great-aunt to tell me that my great-uncle had gone to heaven. I started crying because that was what everyone else was doing.

Two days later, I wore a black band around the sleeve of my white coat when I went with Papa to the funeral. The adults were so emotional with their loss that they didn't realize how confused I was. The house was buzzing with friends and relatives and there in the living room, was Great-Uncle in the casket. Why was he there when he was in heaven? I remember wailing and the strong smell of flowers. I was too young to understand death.

My grandfather, who was also my *parrain* (godfather), held me tightly during the lengthy prayers from the priest and while the box was closed. He had tears rolling down his face as his brother was carried out of the house for the last time. We watched through the window as the men put the casket in a large, horse-drawn black carriage with lamps on its corners, dark red curtains, and filled with funeral flowers.

Suddenly, Grand-Père fell back clutching his chest. A lady whom I did not know pulled me away when my father reached out to help his father. After a while, the lady said, "Emile went to heaven with his brother."

I tried so hard to understand why Grandfather Emile would want to leave me to go with his brother, my great-uncle, who didn't even move any more or smile. It didn't seem fair to me.

A Spunky Fourteen-Year-Old in Love

When I was about fourteen, my friends and I worried about our swimming teacher, who we called Old Mr.

Vanderdam, although he probably was no older than forty-five at the time. He was sick and needed to be away to recover.

In keeping with our young ages, our concern was less about him and more about who would give us swimming lessons. We were told not to worry because Mr. Vanderdam's brother, a Belgian Army captain on leave, would take his place. Then we were anxious, worried about an army officer screaming orders at us as if we were soldiers.

All the way home that day, we talked about what he would look like and if he was married. The next morning, we were in for a big surprise after we sat on the edge of the pool in our ugly black cotton swimsuits that did nothing for our developing figures—except embarrass us.

We could not believe our eyes when this handsome young, blond man showed up looking like something straight out of a Hollywood movie. Immediately we were lovesick. He wore a V-neck tennis sweater over a white shirt and white shorts. Although he supervised our lessons for three weeks, he never once got into the water. And we were so anxious to see him in swim trunks.

We decided it was possible that he didn't know how to swim, even though he was an excellent instructor. I was chosen—or maybe I volunteered—to pretend like I was in trouble in the water. We were sure he would jump in the water to save me. When I thrashed in the water, he just handed me a pole.

We silly girls had another idea. He came behind me on the diving board to position my arms in the proper form for my diving demonstration. As he said, "Go!" I lowered my arm, grabbed his shorts and the two of us hit the water together.

We all laughed hard but then stopped suddenly. What was wrong? I saw the captain gracefully swim to the edge of the pool, his face beet red and his beautiful blond locks floating on top of the water.

He never came back, and swimming lessons were never the same again.

My Teenage Years

After supper when the dishes were done, I often sat on the steps with our neighbor friends, Louisette and her brother, Claude. All the Brouillard kids were impressed with them because, unlike the rest of us, they had traveled a lot. Together we sat talking, solving the problems of the world.

Louisette and Claude's father had been in charge of a rum distillery in Martinique, an island in the eastern Caribbean on the other side of the world. They talked of life so far away from Brussels that it seemed romantic to us, who had never left Belgium. They had servants in Martinique and never had to make their beds, wash dishes, or do chores like we did in Belgium.

Claude, two years older than me, told us wild tales of voodoo rituals. I am sure he exaggerated the facts, but we were ever so willing to believe him. What we did not talk about then was the fact that their father had become an alcoholic and their mother a very unhappy lady.

After our fill of talking, we walked in the dark on the small paths between tall hedges that bordered all the backyards. We were never afraid, as nothing dangerous or violent ever happened in our neighborhood. When we heard the sound of the ice-cream man making his rounds, we knew we neared the end of the walk. The music came from a small music box mounted on the icebox that this very welcomed man pushed in front of his bicycle. We called to him to stop while we rushed to the house to ask for money. We then took our cones back to the steps in front of the house where we resumed talking until Maman called, "Mireille, time to come in!"

Once inside, we washed up and kissed Papa, Maman, and Bobonne good night. We went upstairs to the large room with two double beds that Renee, Angele, Daisy, and I shared. I can still see the furniture, all in mahogany, with elaborate carved headboards. The nightstands and dressers had white marble tops, and a large armoire held our clothes and shoes.

We had so many fun things to do with our friends, we hated it when Maman ordered us to clean that room. Mostly, the younger kids got out of the job, but as the oldest, I could not. An addicted reader, I often sat on the bed reading when I was supposed to be doing chores.

"Mireille, are you cleaning?" Maman called up the stairs.

I made some noise for a few minutes and shouted down, "Yes, I am!" Doing housework was never one of my strong points, and it still isn't.

CHAPTER THREE

THE NAZIS ATTACK

The sound of exploding bombs jerked us awake on the morning of May 10, 1940, which marked the start of the Battle of France, which also included tiny Belgium. We didn't have time to think; we just ran into the street in our nightgowns and pajamas. Seeing overhead German planes dropping bombs on Brussels, we feared for our house. Even if not hit by a bomb directly, a fire could spread to us.

Our house was saved, but Papa found a message in our mailbox. It was a declaration of war from Germany, obviously placed during the night by Fifth Columnists—those who sympathized with the Nazis. According to the declaration, Hitler had no choice but to declare war when Belgium did not give the German Army free travel through the country. It took tremendous organization and a large number of collaborators on the ground in Belgium to place those messages in every postal box.

For adults who had lived through the First World War, horrific memories quickly came back, according to Roger Motz, who wrote: "Immediately, all the dreadful memories of the invasion and the occupation of 1914 were brought back to the minds of Belgians—the massacres at Louvain, Tamines, and Dinant, the shooting of civilians, and then afterwards the four years of misery, humiliation, family and arbitrary executions."[10]

Once the bombing stopped, we went inside, dressed, and learned that all men of fighting age were to report to duty to defend Belgium. That included my forty-one-year-old father, who packed a few things and went away. I cannot tell you how painful that was to see him go. We had no idea when—or if—we would see him again.

The dream was for Belgian men to form an army to fight the Nazis. Living for a time with other men in the cellar of a castle, they had no access to water. He told us they actually washed their feet in wine found there. I bet it was very good wine, but I assume red wine would stain feet.

Some weeks later they came back because it was futile for tiny Belgium to go up against the German war machine. We were thrilled Papa came home safely.

At not quite sixteen, I was the oldest child and had no idea what to do next, but felt an internal drive to do something—anything to defend our small country. Maman, who had been a teenager during World War I, was prepared for the realities of war. She put tape on all our windows to keep them from shattering if the bombs fell again.

She sent the three oldest kids—Andre, Maggy, and me—to buy as many loaves of round, unsliced bread that we could find in every bakery in the area. Younger sisters Angele and Renee were too little to go. I had no idea why she wanted all that bread.

The three of us combed the neighborhood, bringing back probably fifty loaves. She put them in the oven at low temperatures to dry them out until they were hard as nails. My mother wrapped them in cellophane and put them in clean pillowcases that she hung in the attic.

We didn't understand why we did all that until months later when, instead of using the rationed bread literally made of sawdust, she soaked the long-stashed away bread in warm water and plopped it in the oven. Voilà! To our surprise and delight, we had fresh, delicious white bread. Compared to the Nazis' bread it was almost as big a treat as a birthday cake.

With what had been going on in Europe in 1938 and 1939, schoolchildren were given training to prepare for the day that our own country might be forced into another war.

That first day, Girl Scouts handed out rolls and coffee to the men leaving for the front. They would need whatever food we gave them as the German Army was so strong against our small country's tiny forces.

At the start of World War II, the German forces stood in mass on the Siegfried Line on its side of the border, while the French, aided by the Belgians and English land forces, were on the Maginot Line on its side of the border. Ignoring a direct attack on the Maginot Line, the Germans took only seventeen days to cut through Belgium, Luxembourg, and the Netherlands in order to invade France.

In preparation for war, I took medic classes, which involved much more than putting a bandage on a scraped knee. We were taught how to treat war wounds, including removing shrapnel. It was much more extensive care than a young person such as myself would be expected to do, but war was coming. We all knew it.

That first day of the Nazi bombings, I reported to a Red Cross station, ready for excitement. I couldn't wait to see real blood because it was never red in textbooks.

It wasn't long before my dream of seeing red blood came true. Most men in the city, including doctors, were ordered to France to regroup. I worked at the Red Cross Clinic with a nurse or two when injured soldiers started coming to Brussels in droves.

All that was left of one man's shredded hand were pieces of flesh hanging off what was left of his wrist. I assisted the nurse in clamping and tying his blood vessels from what practically was an amputation because that wound had to be cleaned out. Our little clinic had little to ease his pain, having run out of all anesthetics except for cognac. The pain was excruciating.

I came face-to-face that day with the reality of war. I kept up a brave front and was proud and excited to help wounded soldiers. But I was not as tough as I pretended. When I got home, my mother said, "Good. I've kept some soup on the stove for you." One bite and I was really sick. I have never been so sick in my life.

Still, I went back the next day and for many days after that to help that nurse who seemed so old—and brave— at the time to me. I'm sure she was not much older than forty, less than half of how old I am now.

Why did the Nazis care about Belgium? They were most interested in the port of Antwerp on the North Sea, the third-busiest—and highly efficient—port in Europe.

The Nazis knew it would be a great advantage to the British to bring in supplies and weapons through Antwerp. German air raids targeted Antwerp. The German Luftwaffe had set its sights on Belgium's air force, and Deurne Airport in the Antwerp region. The port was another German target. Somehow the port was not destroyed, although much of the rest of the city of Antwerp was severely damaged. The Nazis held it from May 1940 until liberation by the British in 1944.

Beyond the port, Belgium was nothing more to the Nazis than a highway their armies trampled through in Hitler's plan to conquer all of Europe. While occupying our country, the Nazis looted anything and everything they wanted without a moment's hesitation.

The first Nazis to descend on Brussels were the worst of the worst—very cruel and nasty. They loved to shove us around. They raided our museums and banks. They hunted deer with machine guns. They requisitioned—stole—anything they could lay their hands on, including our bicycle and my father's car. If they wanted it, they took it with no recognition of its value or even pretense about our being compensated for our losses. You couldn't argue with them.

Over the coming months, I discovered just how resourceful Maman was. She went to the country to buy butter from farmers she knew. She always walked there and back rather than risk being caught on public transportation. When things got really bad and we did not have coal for cooking, she and her friends walked along the railroad tracks to pick up pieces of coal that fell from trains. When I went out on dates, she drew a "seam" on my legs with an eyebrow pencil to give the appearance of stockings.

When we outgrew our sweaters, she unraveled the yarn, put it into skeins, and then made a new sweater or two. She made us winter coats out of blankets. When it was really cold at night, she put newspapers between our blankets. She also warmed bricks in the oven and wrapped them in towels to put in our beds.

We had so little to eat in those years, but were never really hungry because of Maman's resourcefulness. The Germans took whatever we had, leaving us with ration cards with very small allotments. With her experience in the previous war, she knew how to stretch the food we had—using everything. When she fried bacon—always in small amounts—she took it out from the pan when it was crisp. She then browned onions in the fat and added chopped potatoes, stewing them with water, pepper, and salt. Once it all boiled down, she put the bacon pieces back in, making a real treat on a cold winter night.

Our ration allotted us each one egg a week. Knowing growing kids needed calcium, she dried the eggshell, pulverized it, and mixed it in with whatever we had to eat. It helped provide us with needed calcium in our diet.

I'm sure there were many other brave mothers who managed to keep their children healthy, but I think mine was special. She kept our family going alone during the months that Papa was in France. We were so excited when he and the other men came back. We hugged and kissed him on both cheeks, as was the custom. His return was wonderful and yet ominous—it was futile to fight the powerful German war machine.

As time went on, Maman's forages into the countryside for food became more important—but remained dangerous because they were illegal. The Germans took 90 percent of whatever crops and animals farmers raised. We were lucky to get some potatoes every once in a while. Meat? We had it rarely, if ever.

The Germans, who kept track of everything, insisted farmers report births among their livestock. That way they made sure meat went to their soldiers, not to the starving people who lived in the countries they occupied.

Somehow, my uncle Joseph and Maman were able to buy a baby pig, which was against the German rules. Courageously, Uncle Joseph, the chief electrician at a factory, raised that smelly pig in his basement until it was large enough to be butchered.

One day, the postman knocked at our door with a telegram for us. Normally, a telegram meant only bad news. This time, the telegram said simply, "Uncle Joseph died." I'm sure the postman felt my mother was a very nasty person because she smiled when she read those words. Knowing we would soon get some meat meant it was time to rejoice.

My dad, my mom, Andre, and I each traveled on separate trains to bring back some of the meat. Even if three of the four us of were caught with meat, we figured we'd at least have some for the family. Luckily, we all made it back with our portion of meat. It was so good to have pork again.

My mother remembered the Germans in World War I taking all copper and brass from homes and businesses for production of ammunition. She devised a plan to prevent the Nazis from getting her brass in this war. Maman removed anything in our home made of brass or copper, replacing brass doorknobs with wooden handles. Things made of metal were placed in a laundry basket, stationed at our backdoor. When the Germans came to our front door, I took the basket to our neighbor's back door. Our neighbors did the same when the Germans arrived there, giving their metal or anything else of value to us to hold temporarily. It was easier to do this in Europe than it would be in the United States because houses in Europe were built side to side without lawn between them.

I learned later that the American Army also requisitioned materials from citizens in countries it occupied, like Belgium, but US soldiers at least signed documents promising the materials would either be returned to us, or the people would be compensated for what the US Army took. They followed through with those promises.

CHAPTER FOUR

FIGHTING BACK

Soon after the Nazis came into Brussels, our education became unimportant. Jews were expelled from schools and had no future at all. The rest of us young people were conscripted into war work. I "volunteered" to work at a Brussels factory, hoping to avoid being sent to a labor camp far from my family. I also signed up for night classes, hoping to continue some education, not that the Germans cared whether we learned anything.

A friend and I were assigned to a flashlight factory for German soldiers. Attached to uniform belts like an iPod is carried, each flashlight had a front screen that pivoted so planes flying overhead could not see that light.

We worked in a little room above the factory floor, inspecting the flashlights and boxing them for shipment. We inspected them alright! We secretly took our nail files to work with us and filed down the on/off switch until it was almost out, but not completely. We figured the switch would fall out after a few uses. It was our small contribution to the Allied cause. My father proudly described us as the "destruction department," not the inspection department.

Mary, age sixteen
in 1940, the year
the Nazis invaded
Brussels.

You could say that was when we joined the resistance, working underground. All across Europe there
were people who did what they could to fight back against
the Nazis. Some were in organized groups who met clan-
destinely to share information and figure out ways to
sabotage the enemy. Jews fought back in ghettos and later
in camps, although their opportunities were often small
and extremely dangerous. The United States Holocaust
Memorial Museum described some of these activities:

> In many countries across German-occupied Eu-
> rope, underground partisan units formed to help
> regular Allied forces defeat the Germans. Men

and women joined partisan groups as citizens ful-
filling their patriotic duty to their country or as
members of left-wing (socialist or Communist)
political groups fighting Nazism.

Initially unprepared and disorganized, activities
of resistance groups in the early stages of the war
were usually limited to printing and distributing
clandestine literature, forging passports and other
personal documents, and secretly monitoring foreign radio broadcasts. By 1943, when the war
had turned against Germany, the resistance grew
bolder. Partisans smuggled arms and ammunition
and used hit-and-run tactics to disrupt enemy
communications, kill off isolated groups of German
soldiers, and punish collaborators. Partisans usually lived off the land but were sometimes supplied
with arms and munitions by airdrop. While many
partisans operated illegally from hiding places in
forests, many others worked in urban settings.[11]

I didn't intentionally set out to work in the underground, as frustrated as I was by what was happening in
my country. If you had the right reputation and spirit,
others would know, drawing you into it. For me, it began
with someone asking me to do a little favor. One favor
led to another and another. We sometimes skipped night
class to meet secretly with members of the resistance for
instructions. One day a Belgian man working in my factory quietly asked if I would distribute an underground
newspaper called *Libre Belgique* (*Free Belgium*).

The Belgian people were starved for truthful information that would counter the propaganda that the Nazis fed to them. The Germans took over all of the Belgian newspapers and radio stations, replacing them with their own information machines. Nazi propaganda always proclaimed they were winning the war—even when it was clear that was not the case. Some editors who refused to publish what the Nazis demanded landed in concentration camps and, I assume, lost their lives.

Underground newspapers were the only way that Belgians had kept up with news during World War I, but during World War II, radio reports over the BBC—British Broadcasting Company—were shared. The Nazis forbid us having radios, and the Gestapo—the Secret State Police—even used technology to pick up radio waves as trucks moved through the city. Still, some people courageously listened to the BBC, copying down news that then was printed on mimeographed sheets that became *Libre Belgique* or *La Voix des Belges* (*The Voice of the Belgians*).

These underground papers were important for morale, as Motz wrote in 1942:

> Everything proves that the circulation of underground newspapers is fairly wide, especially as they are passed on quickly from hand to hand. They are much more to Belgians than a source of moral comfort; they represent the assurance, even in the midst of great danger, of the sacred rights to freedom of expression and thought that our citizens will never forego. And that is why hundreds of them, in spite

of severe repression, take part in the printing and distribution of secret newspapers.[12]

The first mimeographed issues that I passed on to family and friends were quite primitive, but by the end of the war, *Libre Belgique* was a real newspaper. Yet just handing out the papers to family and friends wasn't daring or exciting enough for my friends and me.

We rode on the back platforms of streetcars, standing close enough to German officers to stick rolled-up newspapers in officers' overcoats. It was silly and terribly dangerous. Still, we did this because we were determined to show them that people in Belgium resisted what they were doing.

My friends and I collected oak leaf insignia and buttons from Nazi uniforms, quietly cutting them off with razor blades that we carried with us. These buttons and insignia were sometimes gold and sometimes silver, depending on the officers' ranks. Getting them gave us bragging rights much like kids collecting baseball cards. We met at night to announce: "I got four gold buttons today!" Or: "I have three silver buttons!"

We used to tell jokes and stories to keep up our spirits. The one I remember—I forget punch lines—involved Hitler riding in a vehicle driven by a chauffeur who hits a pig on the road. Hitler, supposedly worried about his reputation, sent his chauffeur into the house to pay for the pig. The chauffeur came back with a puzzled look on his face and his arms filled with bottles of wine and hams.

"What's going on? What did they say?" Hitler demanded.

"I don't know, my Führer. I went in and said, 'Heil Hitler. The pig is dead.' They couldn't be nicer."

We were so young that we didn't consider what we potentially were doing to ourselves and to our family and friends. It was dangerous to even tell such a story because there always were people who might be listening without your knowledge. You never knew the sympathies of a nearby stranger or if someone you knew would turn you in for a reward.

Everything I did was risky, and not just for me. The Nazis' rule of terror meant punishing much more than a single person caught in this kind of resistance work. They made examples of that person by torturing and killing this person's entire family or sometimes neighbors.

One night I was asked to deliver a document to a nearby town. I didn't know what it was; it was best if I didn't know just in case I was caught. It was for just this kind of assignment that I enrolled in those night classes. I knew my parents would never let me out at night after curfew except for something like school.

Nazi soldiers stopped me twice that night, but decided this skinny girl in pigtails was not dangerous. They told me to go straight home, and I did. I never had too much trouble those days.

Practically every day under the Nazi oppression, there were new rules, including one that decreed we were to step off the sidewalk and into the street when passing a German. One time, I refused to move when a German officer ordered me off the sidewalk. I still have a dent in my forehead where he hit me with the stock of his gun. He told me I was lucky he didn't shoot me. I went home with blood running down my nose, terrifying Maman.

These activities were a bit like forbidden fruit—irresistible. Telling us not to resist is like ordering kids today not to smoke. Anything banned seems more exciting and foolish to young people who love thrills.

For two years, I continued to pass messages, small arms, and ammunition to members of the underground. My friends and I did other dangerous things just to prove we could. We turned or messed up street signs in the faint hope of misdirecting the advancing Nazis.

We discovered Maman's secret hiding place for our small sugar ration in a locked drawer at the bottom of our living room cupboard. She didn't realize that if you took out the drawer just above it, you could get into the locked one.

Why did we want the sugar? It was not because we had a sweet tooth. We poured sugar into Nazi gas tanks, again hoping to destroy their engines to slow them down. We also slashed their tires.

These were silly, dangerous things to do but represented our very limited way of fighting back. We "showed" the German occupiers that we would not just take what they dished out. This was our country; this was our city.

But it was so little in the face of so much.

Disappearances

The Jewish population of Belgium was historically small. Before World War I, out of a population of around 8 million, there were only 10,000 Jews in the country. However, in the decades before the start of World War II, some Eastern European Jews fled to many places they hoped would be safer, including Belgium.[13] By 1940, there were 35,000 Jews living in Brussels, 55,000 in Antwerp, and another 10,000 around the country.

I remember the many Jewish merchants selling material and clothing on Rue de Haute (Haute Street) in Brussels. Very soon during the German occupation, we heard terrible—and untrue—things said about the Jews who we had known as our friends. We learned how much the Nazis hated Jews, although I still don't understand why.

A directive ordering the wearing of a yellow star by Jews in Belgium in order to easily identify them was announced on May 27, 1942, and came into effect on June 3, 1942. Later, Jewish shops were closed, and by September 1942 we began to hear rumors that some Jews in the neighborhood were being "relocated," while others just disappeared. We had no explanation for why a family would be here one day and gone the next. At this time, we absolutely didn't know about the death and concentration camps.

I learned later that few Belgian Jews who were sent to the notorious death camp, Auschwitz, survived. But I am proud that a smaller percentage of Belgian Jews were murdered than Jews in many other countries. Some Jews might have been protected because the Belgian constitution did not allow a person's religion to be listed on official papers. I know some Belgians turned in Jews to the Nazis, but others hid Jewish children during this terrible time, raising them as if they were their own.

The Nazis were cruel in a way beyond most people's imagination, especially my own. One of their favorite toys was built from two pieces of steel, one placed on top of a prisoner's hand and one underneath. A Nazi interrogator tightened the vise with a big screw that went through the top into the bottom until all fingers were broken. They did other "gentle" things like using pliers to pull out teeth, fingernails, and toenails.

Shortly after the Belgian surrender on May 28, 1940, the Gestapo had taken over Breendonk, a solid old fort on the road between Antwerp and Brussels that dated back to the 1600s. They made the ancient fort into a "reception center" after the Germans invaded Russia in June 1941. But it was really a place of torture for members of the resistance and eventually also for Jews.

If you go to the website for Breendonk, here is some of what you will find:

> Breendonk is only a dot on the gruesome map of concentration camps, but one which witnessed the same desire to annihilate the individual, which shared the same objective of enslaving and negating the human person. . . . Between September 1940 and September 1944, around 3,500 prisoners passed through Breendonk. The majesty of the site and its Dantesque appearance make it a symbol that perpetuates the memory of the suffering, the torture and the death of so many victims. Breendonk, although small in comparison with others, was nevertheless a camp that saw Nazi barbarity sink to its vilest depths.[14]

When Belgian Nazis operated the camp, they greeted prisoners with, "This is hell and I am the devil." And that was what it was—hell. After they tortured prisoners, the Nazis hanged or shot them or sent them to a death camp in the East. More than 3,500 prisoners were housed there over the war years—but no more than 600 at a time.

Breendonk was empty by the time the Allied troops arrived in September 1944. All the prisoners had been forced to other locations or were dead.[15] Breendonk became a national memorial in Belgium in 1947. Since it had been a fort of reinforced concrete, it was fully intact, which meant it could continue to bear witness to what had happened there.

Over those first two years of the war, many of my friends in the resistance vanished. Suddenly, like the Jews, they were simply gone, not there anymore. We heard some Belgian people made it to England, where they regrouped as the Free Belgian forces. This was my dream too. It was crazy, but I was so mad that I felt I would win the war myself.

CHAPTER FIVE

I KNEW I HAD TO GO

After hearing in March 1942 that three of my friends had been caught and undoubtedly had been tortured and/or killed, I decided it was time for me to leave. I did not want to be taken by the Germans or let them hurt my family because of what I was doing.

The night before I left, I got little sleep as I planned my leave. I only had a very small amount of money, borrowed from a friend without telling her how I would use it. I left the house that next morning with a very heavy heart. I could not tell Maman or Papa where I was going or even that I was leaving. If questioned, they needed to be able to say honestly that they did not know where I went. If they had known my plans, I'm sure they would have tried to stop me, fearful for my safety as a young woman. I stopped to see Tante Juliette on my way out of Brussels, but never told her my plans. It was hard to tear myself away.

I knew the only way I could join the Free Belgian forces was to walk from Brussels through France, Spain, and then to Portugal, where I hoped a ship would take me to England. My journey would be 817 miles from

Brussels to Madrid, assuming a direct route, which would be impossible. From Madrid to Lisbon was another 312 miles, again assuming I could walk directly. And then I needed a ship to take me to England. My plans were big and bold—and incredibly naive!

Around this time, there were a number of escape routes for Allied airmen and others fleeing the Nazis. A young Belgian woman, Andrée de Jongh, created the secret Comet Line (Le Réseau Comète), which included safe houses. As her obituary noted in 2007,

> She began, on her own initiative, to organize safe houses to hide downed aircrew and soldiers who had found themselves left behind. It was not long before she started to look for ways of getting them home. From safe houses in and around Brussels, disguised and by different routes, evaders were taken through France to St. Jean de Luz, near Biarritz, close to the Spanish border. From there they were taken on foot through the Pyrenees and over to neutral Spain where they were handed over to British officials. Those helping her as trusted couriers and organizers were often close friends and even members of her own family.[16]

She was known to the soldiers only as Dedée, a nickname for girls named Andrée. She was arrested in 1943, interrogated twenty times, and sent to Ravensbrück Concentration Camp. Other family members, including her father, were tortured and/or killed. The Comet Line most closely matched my path, but it was not until 1943 that the route was actually named as such, according to the World War II Escape Lines Memorial Society. Those who provided assistance along this route were in constant danger.

As the society noted, "The helpers paid a heavy price for returning back to England more than 800 men they had never met before. Over 60% of Comete helpers who had been deported to concentration camps never returned; many were executed or died due to torture, starvation, or beatings. The evaders who had been captured with the helpers were sent to POW camps."[17]

When the Allies liberated these camps, they found some survivors who were very thin, sick, and barely able to walk. "Out of gratitude many evaders supported their helpers in their recovery. Andrée de Jongh later entered into nursing, working mainly in central Africa."[18]

I didn't know all that when I set out to reach the Free Belgian forces on that March day in 1942. I never knew where I was going from one day to the next. Hundreds of people were doing the very same things I was doing across Europe, which made it feel exciting.

As a teenager then, I loved my friends and treasured my family. It's really not much different today—young people want to feel they belong, that they have strong relationships with others.

That need to belong made my work with the underground so difficult. In those terrible days, you never really knew who you could trust and who was an enemy eager to turn you in to the Germans. I could not have friends—not just for my own safety but for theirs as well.

I was very lonely. If I had one person with me all the time I was traveling across Belgium and France, it would have been so much easier for me. I could have shared my fears, and we could plan what our next steps would be. I knew it was too dangerous to travel with anyone. You cannot imagine how alone I felt.

To find myself in resistance work, I needed a certain frame of mind that I would look for and care for others far above myself. I also had to believe that I could do something very important. How did I get this belief? It may have come from Maman telling me about my grandfather's work with the carrier pigeons in the First World War.

I was young and unstoppable—at least in my own head. My dream was to get to Paris to join the Belgian Army. It was a naive idea, but I felt there had to be something I could do in the war, especially after I heard that even Princess Elizabeth of England was doing war work. If the future Queen of England could do that, surely there was something significant for me.

On that morning in March 1942, I left home, with just the clothes on my back. I had on a dress and a coat that had been made for me that year, but it was a summer coat, and because of that, I was miserable in winter.

I walked twenty miles that first day, enjoying the jonquil flowers on the roadside on a bright, sunny spring morning. As beautiful as the day was, it was so hard because my eyes were clouded with tears. That first night I stayed in a convent. The nuns were generous in giving me a clean bed and slices of bread and coffee before I went on the road again.

In those days, you never planned too far ahead. I had been given a place where I would meet my first contact. As I wrote, this man approached me shortly after I sat down by the La Butte du Lion. That man told me where I was to go next and, as usual, we did not exchange names. I was to stop in this or that town and ask for the butcher who would advise me about the next safe contact. After another forty miles or so, I might meet a schoolteacher or a grocer, maybe a minister known to be supportive of the resistance. Each time I arrived at the place where I was to meet my next contact, I prayed this person was still alive and able to help me. This person could just as easily have been a double agent who would turn me in.

My hope as I walked through Belgium was to sleep in a church each night. If I entered before the doors were locked, I could hide and at least spend the night on a pew. That was far better than a barn because I was frightened to sleep in haylofts for fear that mice would run all over me during the night.

Since I didn't have any papers, I had no ration cards allowing me to get the rather dismal allocations the Germans made available. I brought nothing to eat with me, so I often went days without eating. When lucky, priests and nuns allowed me to stay in their convent or church. They never asked why I was on the road; they knew. I also depended on the men I met at night in the woods or my own resources. What I lacked in food, clothing, and money I made up for with determination.

I learned one night that people were not always what they appeared. I stopped at a convent with my usual, "Can

I pass the night? I've lost my way." When I was easily admitted, I thought I was in a safe place. I knew never to say much, but something must have slipped out because this one nun shook her head and said, "This is God's way of doing things. We should not talk that way. It is God's way to turn the other cheek."

Would she think it was God's will to turn me in to the German authorities? I knew I was in dangerous territory.

Brussels was about seventy-five kilometers or nearly forty-six miles from the French border "as the crow flies." My route was much more circuitous as it required going from one contact to another. Sometimes that meant backtracking or taking a side trip, especially if I had something to take to another person. I arrived in France without any problems but had much farther to go.

At Moulins, I reached the demarcation line that separated Free and Occupied France. After France had been invaded and overwhelmed by the Germans, General Henri Philippe Pétain, a French hero during World War I, had negotiated an armistice with the Nazis in June of 1940.

The strategic north and Atlantic coastlines were to be occupied by the Germans, while the rest of the country, Free France with its capital at Vichy, was under the control of the Pétain administration. Pétain became the president and chief of the French State also known as Vichy France. Vichy was actually little more than a puppet state of the Nazis.

Pétain wanted to keep France out of the war, but he was considered a collaborator, something considered traitorous even though he was not as extreme as some of his countrymen. Later, in 1945, as the war was nearing its end, he was urged to flee, but refused, saying his duty was with his fellow French. As the Germans retreated from France in 1944, they arrested Pétain and took him to Germany. The general returned voluntarily to France in 1945. After he was arrested and convicted of treason, he was sentenced to death. French premier Charles de Gaulle, a general who earlier had served under Pétain, commuted his sentence to life. Pétain died six years later in prison.

Today the second largest metropolitan area in France, Lyon played a significant role in World War II. General Charles de Gaulle called Lyon the "capital of the resistance." Some houses of loyalists to the French Republic created secret passages that allowed local people—including members of the resistance—to escape should the Gestapo raid.

That changed in November 1942 when the Germans invaded and occupied Vichy France. I later learned about the brutality of Klaus Barbie, the head of the Gestapo in Lyon. Known as the Butcher of Lyon, he tortured and killed hundreds if not thousands. On April 6, 1944, he personally "arrested" Jewish children hidden in a children's home/school. Most died at Auschwitz, although a few and the school's director were killed by firing squad.

It was in Lyon that I had my close call with the Gestapo, arriving at a safe house as the sirens wailed. It reminded me that I was always one moment away from death, a lesson I learned from the months already on the road and would continue to learn in the months ahead.

At Moulins, I had needed to cross a bridge heavily guarded by Germans that separated the two sections of France. A priest introduced me to a member of the underground, a baker, who decided it was best for me to pass as a worker heading to a job on the southern or free side of the border. The baker gave me temporary use of the identification of his daughter, Paulette. My photo was affixed to her identity card, a horrible counterfeit job, one that should not have passed muster despite his wife changing my hairdo to look more like their daughter's.

My instructions were to walk slowly pushing my borrowed bike from the baker's family in front of me. Rushing would make me appear suspicious to the German guards. My heart beat so hard I was sure they could hear it, but the guard barely looked at the card even though my hand was trembling. It took everything I had to put one foot in front of the other calmly until I reached the end of the bridge. To them, I was nothing more than a harmless, inconsequential little girl, hardly worth their consideration.

On the other side, I saw no swastikas, only French soldiers who proudly flew the French flag. I cried. I felt I was safe now, that the rest of my journey would be so much easier than the three months on the road I had just experienced.

Knowing neutral Switzerland's consulate was the contact for Belgian citizens in France, I went there. A man working for the consulate and the underground provided me with money and directions for how I could get to Spain.

While my confidence grew for a few days, the German invasion and occupation of Vichy France had me back walking from town to town. Only Nazis had vehicles—they had confiscated all privately owned cars. There was no way that I would be offered—or accept—a ride from Nazis!

My little walk proved helpful to the underground because I provided information about German troop movements—but in no way was I a super spy. I simply reported what I saw—the numbers of trucks and what they contained. This information was relayed to the British Broadcasting Corporation and passed on via the radio. The BBC helped people in France and Belgium get word when the war had turned in the Allies' favor, something the Nazis did not want people to know.

I am grateful that the BBC also reported "Squirrel is alive" messages at times. I know my parents heard it at least a few times during the two years I was gone. On occasion, I managed to send unsigned postcards writing about enjoying my vacation "with the barons." It was a reference to German aristocracy.

I was sure that once I made it to the Spanish border, I could easily get to Portugal and then England. First I had to cross the Pyrenees, a range of mountains that were a natural boundary between France and Spain in southwestern Europe. I was referred to a guide who regularly took lost Allied soldiers over the mountains to get back to their own military units.

We were prepared mentally for a long day of climbing, but I was not well equipped for this journey. "The good escaper," says a 1944 British military document called *Tips for Escapers and Evaders*, "is the man who keeps himself fit, cheerful and comfortable. . . . He is not a 'he-man' who boasts about his capacity to endure discomfort. He should be a man with sound common sense and above all a man of great determination."[19]

In November 2011, BBC News Writer Ed Stourton was among those who took that trail in remembrance of those escapers and evaders who had taken this route during the war. "The weather changes as if someone has hit the fast-forward button on the seasons," he wrote. "We experienced dank drizzle, boiling heat, freezing mists, snow underfoot and then more heat in quick succession."[20]

With just one pair of worn shoes my whole journey to that point, I needed basic supplies and equipment to make the trip safely. A resistance worker gave me a dress to replace the one I had worn since I left home and a pair of ski boots for my climb. They were not the stiff boots skiers or climbers use today, but were ankle-high leather—sufficient quality to last the rest of the war.

We climbed for eight hours toward the summit, arriving at Lac Bleu, a glacial lake at an elevation of 6,486 feet overlooking the Lesponne Valley. We had climbed so high that I was quite sunburned, but excited to be at the top and convinced I would soon reach Spain.

Then we saw a group of people coming back toward France. Our guide spoke to their leader, who told him that the Spaniards were paid a bounty to turn in people like us trying to get into Spain over the Pyrenees. If captured, we would be killed or sent to a concentration or death camp.

Sadly, and with great disappointment, we turned back as well. My only choice was to remain in France, working for the Free French, that country's resistance. During this time I met some very nice people, including farmers who helped the war effort by blowing up train tracks.

I also met scary people. I was on a train one day, journeying to deliver messages to another resistance member. The Germans stopped the train, ordering everyone off onto the side. I was carrying messages and had no papers—either of which was sufficient grounds for the Nazis to put a bullet between my eyes.

I can't cry on demand, but I put my hand in front of my face holding my jaw. A soldier asked me what was wrong, and I started crying, really crying. I said I had a terrible toothache. He suggested I go to the first aid station to see if anything could be done to help me. I walked straight into and through that building and kept on going, grateful that I had survived once again. That was really, really close. My looking young and innocent likely saved me again.

D-Day

In 1944, Allied bombing at night was almost a daily event. As frightening as it was to be so near the bombs, we knew each jarring blast was designed to soften up the enemy for the big Allied push that could not come a moment too soon. After four years of war, we were eager but worried. We knew bombs don't discriminate; they hit the innocent as well as the guilty. In one town in the French Alps, I joined many people who went to caves with their mattresses to try and catch some sleep during those frightful nights.

In early June 1944, I was sent to deliver papers to another resistance worker in Normandy, France. I had no idea that I was about to enter the place where D-Day—a most momentous turn of the war—was about to occur on June 6. My eyes opened widely, and I felt such feelings of hope when I saw many, many troops disembarking. We prayed long and hard enough for Germany to lose the war. Was this the answer to those prayers?

The Americans landing was the biggest secret of the war. Only those needing to know were provided that information, and to be eligible for it, their papers had to be stamped with the codeword, "bigot." The Germans had expected the invasion to occur farther east, near the Pas-de-Calais, a reason the Nazis pulled many of their troops out of Normandy. They did so in part because of misinformation given by a double agent known as Garbo.[21] Fake artillery encampments placed as decoys added credibility to the alternative landing site.

On D-Day in World War II—code-named Operation Overlord—some 160,000 US and Allied troops landed on a fifty-mile stretch of beach along the French coastline.[22] In addition, more than 5,000 ships and 13,000 planes were involved in the invasion. Once the Allies took Normandy—after much fighting and the loss of 9,000 men—the Allies marched on through Europe to defeat the German Army.

Just prior to the invasion, General Dwight D. Eisenhower, supreme commander of Allied forces sent this message to his men:

Soldiers, Sailors and Airmen of the Allied Expeditionary Force! You are about to embark upon a great crusade, toward which we have striven these many months. The eyes of the world are upon you. The hopes and prayers of liberty loving people everywhere march with you. In company with our brave Allies and brothers in arms on other fronts, you will bring about the destruction of the German war machine, the elimination of Nazi tyranny over the oppressed peoples of Europe, and security for ourselves in a free world.

Your task will not be an easy one. Your enemy is well trained, well equipped and battle hardened, he will fight savagely.

But this is the year 1944! Much has happened since the Nazi triumphs of 1940–41. The United Nations have inflicted upon the Germans great defeats, in open battle, man to man. Our air offensive has seriously reduced their strength in the air and their capacity to wage war on the ground. Our home fronts have given us an overwhelming superiority in weapons and munitions of war, and placed at our disposal great reserves of trained fighting men. The tide has turned! The free men of the world are marching together to victory!

I have full confidence in your courage, devotion to duty and skill in battle. We will accept nothing less than full victory!

> Good Luck! And let us all beseech the bless-
> ings of Almighty God upon this great and noble
> undertaking.
>
> *Gen. Dwight D. Eisenhower* [23]

I was there by accident at this great moment in history, but I consider it a great honor to have seen it first-hand. It was pure joy to see the Germans retreating with anything they could ride—horses, farm equipment, bicycles, and cars—any form of transportation. As thrilled as we were, we did not dare cheer in the Germans' presence. They would have shot us without a thought.

You can imagine the happiness we felt and how much we did cheer for the Americans when they arrived sixteen days after the Normandy landing. The French people gave the soldiers souvenir handkerchiefs with flags of both our countries printed on them. Having lived under the tyranny of the Nazis for years, the French people would have done anything and given anything to the Americans to thank them for their liberation.

But the fighting was not over where I was in the Normandy area—it lasted for two months and only ended with the liberation of Paris on August 19, 1944. At one point, I was in a field with about twenty-five refugee children and adults. We had all congregated there, a few miles from the beach, trying to stay away from the shooting. We kept our heads down because we were caught between the Americans in a church steeple shooting down on German soldiers in the road and the Nazis firing back on the Yanks.

Never before had I seen the trace of bullets going past me. It was then we realized that the Americans didn't know we were in that field. Two of us climbed to the top of the hill, crawling quietly to tell the soldiers there were refugees in that field. This was not heroic— just self-preservation.

As the end of the war neared, there would be more and more refugees trying to find places for themselves after being forced from their homes. Estimates were that there were from 11 to 20 million displaced persons in Europe after the war with no homes, families, or places to go.

I eventually met two American flyers, who introduced me to soldiers of the American Army Counterintelligence Corps (CIC). I joined them, serving as a translator as they rounded up people suspected of collaborating with the Germans and Nazis in hiding. The soldiers took me under their wing and used me to help identify local people trying to hide their complicity.

We all stayed in a house in Normandy once occupied by the Gestapo. The next-door neighbors told us that they had seen Nazis digging in the yard. An American officer ordered German prisoners of war to dig up the backyard. There they found the body of a secretary who had worked for the resistance. The Gestapo tortured her, killing her with electric shock so powerful that her arms and legs were out of joint. They then buried her in the backyard.

The US soldiers insisted I stay away from the house's basement, without telling me why. But being really nosy, I went down there and learned the reason they tried to protect me. On the walls were meat hooks, and there were bloodstains all over the basement. This place where the Gestapo had interrogated prisoners showed signs of unimaginable brutality that they didn't want me to see.

During my work in the underground, I carried small guns, ammunition, and occasionally dynamite, but I never fired a weapon until a couple of American soldiers talked me into it. It would be so easy, they told me. All I had to do was aim. The gun had such a powerful retort that I landed on my seat, much to the soldiers' amusement. At just over five feet in height, I was definitely not built to fire a gun.

Compared to the rest of us, the American Army ate very well—even when away from their mess kitchens. They carried C-rations, which came in cases weighing seven pounds. Each had six rations consisting of twelve-ounce cans of bread, instant coffee, and sugar; twelve-ounce cans of meat and vegetables; and cigarettes, toilet paper, gum, and candy.[24]

Beginning in 1942, many soldiers received K-rations—individual daily combat rations that held three meals: breakfast, lunch, and supper. They had more variety and were not as heavy as they were designed for paratroopers.

After a month of C-rations, K-rations seemed like a banquet to me but did not appeal to the American soldiers who were accustomed to better fare. We had a cook with our unit who found a way to make clever meals out of these limited ingredients. Once in a while we even had a fresh vegetable requisitioned from a farmer or bartered for cigarettes or coffee.

Rarer, we had an even better treat—pork chops if a pig somehow got run over by accident on the road. Since that kind of accident only happened at night, the soldier could not find the farmer. He had no choice but to put the pig in the back of the Jeep. There was no reason to waste a perfectly good pig, was there?

One day someone suggested we catch some fish, but we had no equipment and little time to sit along a river waiting for something to bite. Then a week later, the answer came in the form of a cache of German grenades. The soldiers didn't speak French and I didn't speak English, but they motioned me to go with them to the river.

German grenades were like bottle grenades with handles. I stood on a bridge where, on their signal, I threw a lit grenade in the water. Boom! Stunned fish floated up the surface ready to be harvested by my friends with makeshift nets. It was not very sportsmanlike, but we shared a wonderful dinner. That's war.

The CIC unit's captain, who called me "Little Chickadee," was especially kind to me even though he did not speak French. But he did pick up some French slang, promising me the American Army would get the Boche. This derogatory term for Germans came out of World War I after being shortened from *alboche*, which combined Allemand (German), and *caboche* (cabbage), a food the Germans were known to eat.

Another time, the men in the counterintelligence detachment tried to communicate with me about what we were having for dinner. That same captain worked an English-French dictionary without luck. Then he got a big grin on his face and announced to me in French—*la mère de l'oeuf*—"mother of the egg!" We were having chicken.

The soldiers were determined to teach me English, but their lessons were ones that I mostly had to forget when I discovered what I was learning from them. They thought it was the funniest thing in the world to teach me nasty words. I had to clean up my language later when I took a job with the US Army in Frankfurt, Germany.

Back to Belgium

In September 1944, I was thrilled to learn Canadian troops and then British troops had reached and liberated Belgium, including Brussels. In a letter to his sister, Vera, Canadian soldier Frank William Clarke described the liberation as "the greatest advance in history."[25] In that letter, which was posted on the World War II People's War online archive of wartime memories, he said their assignment was to cross the River Seine. He wrote about liberating town after town in great excitement, but with little sleep. They learned one Saturday night that they would travel ninety miles the next day to Brussels to liberate that city.

> On and on we drove towards Brussels, the excitement getting more intense every hour. The people were getting frantic! The route was a blaze of colour and my arm fair ached with waving to the excited crowds. At times it was almost impossible to move through the seething masses, for they climbed on to the trucks kissing us and crying. These people had been four years beneath the Nazi

yoke, suffering, unhappy and now they were free. The Allies had fulfilled their promise. Liberation was theirs. . . . As we neared the centre of the city, progress got very slow for the crowds were blocking the roads. The whole of Brussels had come out to welcome us.

Mary on her way back to Brussels from Frankfurt, Germany, where she worked briefly for the US Army after the war.

Clarke told his sister that they found thousands and thousands of bottles of wine and champagne that the Germans hid in the Palace of Justice. When the soldiers brought up the wine, "Brussels fairly swam in wine. The celebration was tremendous."

Meanwhile, I was still with that US Army CIC outfit, which also hoped to reach Germany. They thought it was too dangerous for me to continue on with them, but I objected. I had spent years in the resistance and underground fighting the Nazis. I was tough and not afraid. I wanted to be there for the Allies' victory inside Germany.

Still, the captain insisted it was too dangerous and dropped me off at my parents' home. Maman and Papa were not home for that reunion, but my grandmother was. She almost fainted when she saw me and then covered me with kisses, back and forth on my cheeks, as is the custom. When Maman came home, she took one look at me and said something like, "I am so angry at you, but I'm so glad you are home."

When I think about what I put my parents through, I feel terrible. It was an awful thing to do, leaving them without a word. But war is an awful thing. If I were my parents, I would have killed me for the many actions I took in the resistance. I had put all of them at risk, and I'm sure they worried constantly. I noticed my mother lost a lot of weight while I was gone—food was not plentiful, but I'm sure her fears about me added to the loss. This is the point of my story when I tell it, that I say to my kids not to try anything like this.

Mary back in Brussels after the war.

Despite those rare radio transmissions, "Squirrel is alive," and an occasional postcard saying I was "having a wonderful time with the barons," they rightfully worried. I think to never know where I was or even if I was dead or alive was horrific. It is something that I only appreciated after becoming a parent myself.

It was not easy for my parents because the Germans kept detailed records of every single person in the cities they occupied. People couldn't just disappear without an investigation—unless the Gestapo took them away. I thought when I left that I was saving my family because they would have been tortured and killed if their daughter had been caught working in the underground. In leaving, I still put them at risk as they had to endure the interrogations of the Gestapo about where I was. My mother convinced these brutal secret police that I had run away from home, and she had no idea where I was.

Mostly during the war my family carried on, doing the best they could with much less and the constant fear that the Gestapo would return to ask more questions about me or take any valuables not hidden in time. It was a life of constant uncertainty.

I was amazingly lucky to have survived two years on the road as a young, attractive woman. Perhaps I was too dirty to be of interest to men along the way. It certainly was a different time in terms of the courtesy given to a young girl.

It was all so long ago—nearly seventy years—and I still shake my head at the thought of leaving home as a young girl without preparation and only a snapshot of my family. I didn't consider practical issues, such as food and shelter, let alone the question that a nun asked me privately after hearing me speak a few years ago. She wanted to know how I handled my monthly period. I told her frankly that while some women might have stopped menstruation under those circumstances, I continued to flow. Mostly I pilfered towels hanging out to dry that I cut up and later threw away.

When a member of the resistance was arrested, the Nazis served up revenge that went far beyond that prisoner. For example, the response from the Nazis on June 9, 1944, to the resistance taking over a town and killing forty Germans was to round up 130 men to be executed, although only ninety-nine were killed that day. Some bodies were left hanging on lampposts and balconies and sixty-seven others were killed in Argenton-sur-Creuse, also in France.

Days after D-Day, the Nazis on June 10, 1944, killed 642 men, women, and children and then burned the village of Oradour-sur-Glane in west-central France. When we heard about these massacres it frightened us, but it also made us more determined to fight back.

It was an honor to hear how important General Eisenhower felt our work was. On an Order of the Day on October 2, 1944, he praised the work of the Belgian resistance.

> Now that the soil of Belgium is almost liberated, I wish as Supreme Commander of the Allied Expeditionary Forces to pay sincere tribute to the officers and men of the resistance groups who in carrying out my orders, have fought magnificently. They can be justly proud of having by their devoted heroism contributed so largely to the liberation of their beloved homeland. The rapidity of the advance of the Allied Forces which has spared much of your country the horrors of war has been due in no small measure to your help. I salute especially your honoured dead and wounded.
>
> The success, which has attended our arms, has led us out of Belgium into other theatres of operations. Fighting is therefore over for most of you as soldiers of resistance groups. This does not

necessarily mean that your services are no longer needed. The war is being carried into the enemy's country, and if you are required by your government to continue the struggle as members of the regular Belgium Armed Forces, I shall be proud to have you once more under my command.

Meanwhile, in my capacity of Supreme Commander, I wish to say to the soldiers of the resistance groups that those of them who are no longer engaged in fighting or on guard duties etc., upon orders of the Allied Commanders, can best assist the military effort by handing in their arms to their authorities and awaiting their instructions as to how they can best play their part in the struggles ahead. These arms are urgently needed for other purposes.

Until hostilities cease, all activities, whether in the workshop or at the front, must be directed against our common enemy.

In his book, *Crusade in Europe*, Eisenhower wrote, "Throughout France the Free French [that is, the Resistance] had been of inestimable value in the campaign. . . . Without their great assistance the liberation of France and the defeat of the enemy in Western Europe would have consumed a much longer time and meant greater losses to ourselves."[26]

CHAPTER SIX

REJOINING THE AMERICANS

I was happy to be back with my family again, but life in the city, particularly in my parents' home and Brussels felt so dull after two years of being on my own. When I came home, my parents wanted to keep me back under their wing. They missed me and wanted to make sure I didn't go away again.

I imagine it is what college students feel like when they come home for summer after their first year of being away. They are bored and struggle against being held under the rules they had as high school students. I was used to making my own decisions, even ones that, looking back, were crazy.

Wanting to do something to help the Americans now occupying the city, I applied to work at an enormous ordinance company in the Brussels suburb of Forest. Located on a large sand quarry, this is where the US Army inspected Jeeps and trucks returned from the front lines. After a vehicle's inspection, reports were turned over to me to figure out repair costs.

I never could understand why we went to all this trouble. The US government paid for it all, but still everything had to be typed in six copies. I was sure this infinite paper trail cost more than the repairs. Occasionally, when a vehicle needed repairs because of negligence of a soldier or airman, I performed some creative computations so the serviceman did not have too much coming out of his pay.

◀ Mary in 1945 or 1946 in the US Army ordinance depot near Brussels where she did clerical work immediately after the war.

Mary (right) stands on one of the vehicles under repair in the depot. Beside her is her sister or another worker.
▼

Meeting My Husband

As one of only two women working for the 686 Ordinance Unit, we had many opportunities for dates, but no one caught my interest. Then when coworker Paula was going out one night with a soldier, she suggested I go out with this staff sergeant, Allen Rostad, on a double date.

We went to G.I. Joe, a nightclub run by the USO, where we sipped white wine, enjoyed the big band, and fell in love over the song "Stardust." After that, we talked a lot and went out a few times. When Allen visited my parents' home, my brother and sisters looked up to him as a big brother. Maman and Papa did not have much to offer except their hospitality. Food was still hard to find, but Allen and I went to a little restaurant at the Grand Place St. Dennis, the city center, for fish and French fries. Or, we went to a butcher shop for steak tartare, after Allen got over the shock of eating "raw meat."

After his unit was transferred to Butzbach, Germany, about twenty-two miles north of Frankfurt, we wrote every day, letters I'll let my kids read after I've gone to heaven. After several long months of being separated from him, Allen came to visit for Christmas and asked me to marry him.

I did not want to be apart from him any longer, so I applied to work for the Criminal Investigation Command, known as the CIC. As part of the application process, I took a physical exam. I stripped down, wrapped myself in a sheet and then went into the room where I thought the doctor would see me. Instead, I walked into the wrong room where there were four completely naked men! I quickly backed out of there.

Learning About Atrocities of War

I passed inspection and was given a job in the IG Farben building in Frankfurt, which had become the headquarters for the United States Army and General Eisenhower after World War II. IG Farben was part of the Nazi war machine, creating synthetic oil and rubber during the war and most horrifying, Zyklon B, the gas that was used in the death camps to kill millions of Jews and others. General Eisenhower changed the building name to the United States Force European Theater.

The CIC's work involved investigation of Nazi war crimes against humanity. That's where I finally learned about all of the horrors of the Nazi regime. I wrote summaries of what had happened at the concentration and death camps, something even I in the resistance did not know.

Shock and horror do not begin to describe my reactions—and those of Americans—when men started telling stories about what they had seen. One man came in with lampshades and billfolds that had been made out of the skin of Jewish prisoners.

According to the Virtual Jewish Library, it was Ilse Koch, the wife of the commandant of Buchenwald, who was accused of making human-skin ornaments, including lampshades,. She was twice convicted of war crimes, including cruelty to inmates and murder, but it was not proven that she had made the lampshades herself.

> It's exceedingly well-documented that such ornaments did exist; there's no question but that someone made them out of human skin. When

one can see a book whose cover is tanned skin with a decorative tattoo on it, there's little question that the skin was that of a human being. If one has any doubt as to the origin of the substance, one should examine the forensic report conducted on some of the skin. It concludes, based on microscopic examination and the placement of the nipples and navel, that the skin was certainly human.[27]

General Eisenhower wanted the German population—many of whom claimed not to know about these camps—to be made aware of horrors done in their names. He ordered German citizens be taken to concentration camps or to movie theaters where films of the camps were shown to see evidence of these gruesome crimes.

I visited one of these camps and will never forget what I saw. Rooms assigned to hold belongings that prisoners brought were filled with dentures, eyeglasses, shoes, and other property taken from prisoners.

How do you put into words what it means to see a room filled with women's hair? You knew that this hair came before or after the deaths of countless innocent people. Why did the Nazis shave hair of prisoners when they arrived in these camps or after they were gassed?

They wanted to cause fear and shame in prisoners, take away their individuality and demonstrate their absolute domination over those who were to be worked to death rather than gassed. The Nazis also had a use for all that hair. Since human hair does not age or deteriorate, it was stuffed into life vests and mattresses, and later put in soldiers' blankets.

Before the Allies liberated Brussels, my mother saw German trucks come into the city with 10,000 pairs of children's shoes, undoubtedly from 10,000 children who had been killed. The Nazis didn't waste much; they took the clothes from all these dead people and brought them back for their own. You can't digest that much horror, particularly learning about people who enjoyed causing so much pain.

One action that I learned about while working in that building was so horrible that I blocked it from my mind. When the resistance killed two German soldiers, the Nazis took revenge by hanging civilians from the balcony of their headquarters. Most of my friends who disappeared from Brussels during the two years I was there under the Nazi occupation never came back.

When I was with the resistance, I personally witnessed Nazis rounding up Jewish people in one village, taking the men away by truck. Moments later we heard the machine gun fire and knew what it meant—and so did the Jewish women who quickly gave away their babies to French strangers because they knew they were next to be killed. These were not isolated incidents; I later learned about SS-Einsatzgruppen who operated in Eastern Europe. They traveled as mobile death squads from village to village to kill whole towns of Jews, who first had to dig their own mass graves. Death camps with gas chambers and cremation in Poland took over for the Einsatzgruppen because shooting whole towns of people was not efficient enough to wipe out all the Jews in Europe.

This extent of Nazi hatred for Jews was not something that I understood then or even now. We should have known what they planned to do and fought back, a reason that many of us still beat ourselves because of our guilt. But nothing had ever happened like these mass roundups and killings before in world history. How could we know and yet how could we not know?

In Belgium, many Christian families took in Jewish children, raising them as their own to save them. Can you imagine giving up your child? I found that so horrific, but everything about this was nasty and cruel.

In Germany, the army provided me with a home to share with three other young women working for the US government. It was a life so different from what I had experienced the previous four years. A German woman cleaned our home, drew our baths, and washed our clothes. We were not supposed to talk with her—just give her orders. She was really nice, so it was hard not to fraternize with her. We were not supposed to give her anything, but I casually left my chocolate ration around the house, hoping her kids would get it.

You never really knew the sympathies of the German people. We were told about one woman who had provided daycare to Jewish children, only to turn them over to the Nazis. It was hard not to hate the Germans after all we had gone through and learned about through the work I did. Some were just following orders or did things with a gun to their heads. But maybe there were others who could have said "No!" and fought off this madness.

I still have nightmares about what I saw and learned in those years, including about the cruel medical experiments conducted on twins. How could I forget?

Living in a Fairytale

IG Farben made tremendous money as war profiteers, enough so that their headquarters, the magnificently beautiful I.G. Farben complex, had forty elevators. The army provided us with all our meals in the building, where the dining rooms had crystal chandeliers and marble floors. The tables were set with crystal, Limoges china, and sterling silver. String quartets entertained us over breakfast and lunch, and dinner always was formal and followed by dancing.

After years of being deprived, I was living in a fairy tale.

The work was not hard, but we produced many lengthy reports of war criminals and spies. The pay was generous and the perks a wonder. I had a Jeep at my disposal any time I wanted with a prisoner-of-war driver. Most of my trips took me to Butzbach to see Allen.

His friends were always happy to see me because I turned over my daily liquor ration to them. Since they were enlisted men, they could only buy one drink at a time at the Post Exchange, or PX.

There was such a difference between Allen's camp and my own quarters. His barracks were clean and dry and they had good food, but the camp itself was one big mud field. I can still remember the sign at the entrance of his unit: "This is your home. Keep it clean." That was not easy under those conditions.

Mary after the war in 1946. She is wearing her future husband's service ribbon.

Wedding Plans

My parents and siblings loved Allen. My sisters often sat on his lap and my parents were impressed with his kindness. They were happy to hear we would marry, although I'm sure they would prefer we lived in Belgium than the United States. I had fallen so much in love with America that I was willing to go to the States with Allen—no question about that—even if we did not marry until I arrived.

We thought we had the documents needed to marry in Brussels in March 1946, including the chaplain's paperwork. But Allen's captain blocked his weekend pass, calling his getting married a "lousy idea." Proving again I had spunk, I went to see the general in charge of the Seventh Army who was based in the same building as I was. More than understanding, he made a phone call to get the furlough approved and offered us his best wishes.

Allen Rostad and Mary, in a military jacket for a wedding dress, on their wedding day, March 16, 1946.

Lieutenant Dybing, who had long been a friend of both of us, gave Allen the use of a Jeep for the weekend. A day later we arrived in Brussels, where we learned we could not be married in the church because the priest said the "banns had not been posted for six weeks" as required by the Catholic Church. The banns were public pronouncement of our intention to marry that would allow people to object if they felt the wedding should not go on. Asked if the banns could be lifted, the priest said, "Yes, by the pope."

So we made the decision to have a civil wedding, but even that had its problems. The banns still needed to be published four weeks before a civil ceremony could be held. This time we did not need the pope's approval—just proof that Allen was to be sent back to the United States.

On March 14, 1946, we went to Antwerp, where the acting assistant adjutant general signed a document that said Allen's furlough was canceled. He was to return to his unit in Butzbach, Germany, by March 18, 1946, because he was being sent back to the United States. That gave us the weekend to marry, which we did on Saturday, March 16, 1946, in the courthouse.

Every girl dreams of wearing a white wedding gown on her wedding day, but in this case the bride wore khaki—my uniform as a Belgian civilian personnel attached to the US Army. Yes, no white dress and veil—only khaki down to and including my underwear.

I still have my tiny military jacket that carried the Galleries Lafayette label inside. We had to wear our uniform all the time—including to my wedding. This jacket was so small—I was absolutely tiny then having gone through two years of very little food.

After the wedding, Allen and Mary can't take their eyes off each other, while Mary's parents (on the right) seem to be thinking of losing their daughter to America.

The *maire*—mayor—read the wedding ceremony in French, which I translated word by word to Allen. We then walked back to our house for toasts, a dinner, and lots of laughing and singing. My brother, Andre, and his friends decorated the Jeep we took to get to the home of Uncle Joseph and Aunt Renee for our brief honeymoon—they stayed with my parents so we could be alone. After two happy days on our own, we went back to Germany to our units.

Allen left for the United States on a troop ship at the end of April, but I had to wait until May 19 to join him. It seemed like forever.

Coming to America

The railroad station was crowded with happy people, those going and those seeing them off. I was happy, too, but also sad because it all happened so quickly. I was leaving my family once again after just three days in Brussels to say goodbye. Maman shopped with me to make sure I had decent civilian clothes, including new shoes, underwear, and all things a bride needs.

During those last moments before I boarded the train, Maman, Papa, Grandmother, Andre, Daisy, Angele, Renee, and I stood on the platform trying hard not to cry. We had been back together such a short time. As we were growing up, Andre and I as the oldest were always in competition with each other—typical sibling rivalry. I missed the years when he grew to become a man. My sisters were so little when I left and they, too, were growing fast.

We promised each other that we would see each other soon, although we knew that would be very difficult. As the train started and I waved goodbye, I felt the tears rolling down my cheeks. I cried for a long time.

In Paris, we war brides were taken to a hotel that night that was close enough to my cousins to visit them before I left. Cousin Rene took us back to the hotel after our brief reunion.

Then fifty of us took the train to Camp Philip Morris—yes that Philip Morris; each of the debarkation camps in France was named after a tobacco company. From the camp, located near the port city of Le Havre, France, we boarded our ship. Le Havre had been severely damaged by the Allied bombing during the Battle of Normandy, but we never saw the damaged parts of the city.

We boarded the USS *George S. Goethel*, a Liberty Ship that was a troop transport during the war. It was named after Goethel, who earned a Silver Star during World War II. This slow-moving steamship—no luxury liner—was reassigned to ferry 400 war brides and some children to the United States. Most of us were excited, happy, and a bit nervous about what our new country would be like.

But among us were at least fifty young women who survived years in concentration camps all over Europe. They were so thin and ill from their horrific experiences, and frightened about what was ahead. Having lost their families in these camps, some may have married the first men who offered them security.

Some of the women who later would be called Holocaust survivors self-consciously tried to cover the numbers tattooed onto their arms in Auschwitz. The perpetrators of these crimes were the ones who should feel shame, not these women. Later I learned some survivors wore special jewelry to mask their number or had their tattoos removed by plastic surgery. I'm sure that must have been painful.

Because I still wore a uniform of a Belgian civilian working for the Allies and had served with the US Army, boat officials assumed I knew much more than I did about the United States. They made me the liaison for 200 of the war brides. I was supposed to talk with these women to learn if they had any problems or needs and then to work with the Red Cross staff to resolve their concerns.

The crew and Red Cross staff worked very hard to make us feel comfortable on this ship, but it was not easy. Half the brides were seasick that first day—and many for days longer—holding on to the railing for support. We also had sick babies and GI brides who because of language difficulties could not make their needs understood, particularly if they were Slovak nationals. None of us knew their language.

I had still another role. A Protestant minister conducted religious services, but with no priest on board, I was asked to lead Catholic Church services each morning. I did so proudly. We all prayed for safe travels and a better life in America.

In the afternoons, I helped arrange entertainment for the war brides, based on the talent we had on board—a pianist who won first prize in a competition with the Paris Conservatory, ballet dancers, and singers with voices like angels. With limited resources, we recruited scarves from passengers for the dancers to wear as costumes.

Each show ended with singing "The Star-Spangled Banner," the national anthem of the country we would soon call our own. It brought tears to the eyes of the ship's captain to see us embrace this anthem and his country.

We arrived in New York on May 26, 1946, after traveling 3,306 miles from Le Havre. As we entered the port we saw "her"—the Statue of Liberty—standing tall, her arm held high. Seen from the ocean, Lady Liberty took our breath away because she was so welcoming to us. Once on shore, many sobbing brides dropped to their knees and kissed the ground. America symbolized opportunity and hope and they had gone through so much.

We stayed in port for a day for medical exams, delousing, money exchange, and verification of documents. That night we noticed only half of the crew remained on the ship, which meant the rest must have gone ashore. Three of us brave-but-foolish wives felt we had to see New York City, which we had long heard and read about back in our own countries.

The ship's captain could not drink a drop of alcohol while his ship was at sea. But once in port, he imbibed to his heart's content. He was well lubricated when we approached him about giving us a pass to see the city. In his drunken state, he agreed.

We hailed a New York cabbie, who agreed to drive us all over town when he learned we were war brides. This man, who had an accent himself, gave us the grand tour—taking us from the amazing bright lights of Broadway to the Italian and Chinese neighborhoods and to everything in between. After about three hours, he took us back to the ship and refused payment by saying, "Welcome to America." His accent told us he had once been an immigrant to the United States. We were so excited that night that we could not sleep back in our staterooms.

The next morning, we were escorted to the train station and sent on our way to the towns and cities where we would find our husbands. It was hard to leave these women I had known for about ten days, but my adventure with my new husband in this place called Minnesota awaited. I had never heard of Minnesota before I met Allen, but I have always been game for something new.

We all wore tags around our necks with basic information, including where we were going and our husband's name. You would think we were being sent off to camp or boarding school. The Red Cross arranged for and paid for our transportation.

Coming from Europe, we were amazed by the wide-open spaces of the United States and the distances between cities and towns. Even between countries in Europe, travel takes so much less time. Of course, European cities went back much further, hundreds of years older than those in America.

Over the three days or so on the train to Chicago, we were excited and hopeful for each other as each one reached her destination. I rode to Chicago, Illinois, and then took another train to La Crosse, Wisconsin, which is just across the Mississippi River from Minnesota. Since Allen's address was in the town of Yucatan in Houston County, the Red Cross arranged for him to pick me up in nearby Spring Grove.

To get to Spring Grove, I boarded a train that looked like a relic of many years gone by. The conductor apologized, telling me that this freight train had not seen a passenger in ten years. With its dusty red velvet seats and oil ceiling lamps, I felt like I was riding in an old Hollywood Western. Out my window, I expected to see the cavalry fighting Indians—images from the movies I had in my head of America outside of New York City.

It practically took longer to ride the thirty miles from La Crosse to Spring Grove, Minnesota, than it did from Chicago to La Crosse. We stopped at many towns to take on water, and each stop seemed longer than the time we were moving.

I was very tired but excited when I finally reached Spring Grove because I saw Allen standing at the station. We kissed, hugged, and held on to each other, hardly believing we were finally together.

He introduced me to his brother-in-law, Gerhardt, husband of his sister, Leona. Gerhardt insisted we stop at a tavern for a beer. We then went to the home of Allen's sister Viola and her husband, Rolland, who lived in a small house next to their store in the township of Yucatan.

Everything was so different, so strange. I was now living in a very small town after growing up in Brussels, a metropolitan city that today has well over a million people. Everyone in Allen's family appeared welcoming, but it was overwhelming. Allen and I needed to escape into the hill behind the house to catch our breath.

We stayed with Viola for three days and then moved to the home of Gladys and Leo, another sister-in-law and brother. There we slept on a sofa in their living room for way too long.

Millions of military men had returned from war expecting to get back to their lives and to start their families. Housing was extremely tight because little construction was done during the Great Depression and World War II. Jobs also were hard to come by.

Finally, there was a break for us—a little guesthouse was for sale, but it had to be moved from its location. Luckily, the Houston Town Board offered us land next to the town hall as a site for the cottage. All they wanted in exchange was for us to make coffee and sandwiches when they held meetings.

The cottage had one big room and a small, attached closet. It was very pretty, was freshly painted inside, but it had no water or bathroom—we used the town hall's outdoor facilities. It seems impossible today to be satisfied with such a house, but we were thrilled because it was a place of our own where we could finally be alone.

We had nothing in the way of furniture even for that tiny little place, so we went to La Crosse and bought a table, four chairs, a dresser, sleeping sofa, and a kerosene stove. We divided our closet into two sections—one for clothes and the other for the water supply that Allen fetched from across the road.

We moved our little cookstove in and out of the closet depending on the season. We used the town hall's outdoor toilet as our own. It really was like we were just playing house.

We made do with much less than young people have now, but those were the times. Most of us had grown up during the Depression and World War II when we had even less. Neither one of us was very demanding. We lived in that house when our first son, Andre, was born in 1947. Thank goodness it was large enough for a crib. We wanted only the best for him—so we bought him a new crib, a high chair, and a playpen.

When Andre was almost two, we moved to a small house that gave us more room but still did not have an indoor bathroom. We did have a regular bed, a stove, and a refrigerator. That was living—but I still miss our first little house sometimes.

After a few small jobs, Allen began working in the local hardware store in Houston, Minnesota, his job for more than thirty years. He then was an appliance repairman on his own for another ten years as Rostad Home Repair.

Unofficially he retired many times. But he was not the kind of man who could say no when someone needed help. He had heart surgery in 1994 but recovered and continued working for a long time when people in Houston called for him.

Becoming a Nurse

Working in the underground in France, I loved caring for people who were wounded or ill. I used some of those medical skills I gained as a teenager in Brussels, although I knew I could never become a doctor as I once dreamed. After the war, I had a new country, a husband, and soon a family.

My skills also came in handy when our daughter, Denise, was hospitalized to have her tonsils removed. As was the style in Belgium, I stayed with her in the hospital, helping to care for her, something that was natural for me. Nurses at Lutheran Hospital in La Crosse were so impressed that they asked me where I had my nurse's training. I told them about the work I had done so many years ago in France and Belgium. They suggested I work at the hospital, saying, "We can really use the help."

The next week I was a nursing assistant in what is now Gundersen Lutheran Medical Center in La Crosse.

I stayed there for thirty years on a floor that primarily cared for neurosurgery patients. Later, I became a licensed practical nurse, but declined the opportunity to become a registered nurse. I wanted to do bedside nursing, not paperwork, which is what so many RNs seemed to be doing. After thirty years full time, I worked part time another ten years and was on-call twenty-four hours a day for enucleating, which is the removal of eyes that are donated after death.

I valued most caring for my patients in my nursing career—helping them to feel better. Sometimes I bent and stretched the rules just a bit if I thought it would benefit my patients. I would round up and store food—sometimes in the ceiling—in case a patient became hungry later. I also saved other supplies that would prove helpful at night when we couldn't just run to central supply.

Returning to Belgium and France

I didn't get back to Europe as often as I liked because we had very limited resources while we were raising our family of three children. I actually was embarrassed into going the first time. My mother and my aunt came to see us in Houston a year or so before I went there. If these elderly women could make the trip in the late 1970s, I certainly could too.

My first trip back to Belgium was in 1977 with our son Kim. It was our graduation present for him after graduation from Western Wisconsin Technical College, now called Western Technical College. I took a couple other trips by myself and then traveled with my daughter, Denise, in 2006 and 2010.

When we visited my family in 2006, we drove to nearby Luxembourg to visit the American Cemetery just over the border into that tiny country. Arriving in late afternoon, we heard the sound of "Taps" being played. We froze in our tracks. That music combined with the solemn beauty of rows of white crosses on a field of green grass, reminded us we were on sacred ground.

It was the final resting place of 5,706 Americans, many lost during the Battle of the Bulge, the last-ditch effort of the Nazis to get back territory it lost in Western Europe. Brutal winter weather hampered the US forces, but still the line against the Nazis only "bulged," instead of breaking. That is why it was called the Battle of the Bulge. Those 5,706 were a small percentage of the astounding 75,000 American men and up to 100,000 German casualties.[28]

After that trip, Denise described our experiences to some friends in Platteville, Wisconsin, where she teaches. She learned the first husband of her friend's mother was buried in an American cemetery after his plane was shot down during a mission.

When we returned in 2010 to visit family, we took a car trip to Neupré, near Liège, the site of the Ardennes American Cemetery. Near the southeast edge of Neupré (formerly Neuville-en-Condroz), this cemetery was the final resting place of 5,328 soldiers buried on 90.5 acres, including 792 whose identities remain unknown. We drove through the gate and down a long road to the visitor's center, which we found to be dignified and adorned with photos of United States presidents. In signing the guest book, we learned the last visitors had been from

Minnesota as well. With a page from the cemetery's website showing the section, row, and number of the site, we followed the map into the cemetery.

The vista of the memorial—gravestones, the green grass, and the American flag—were all breathtaking. When we approached the huge white memorial, we talked with the visitors from Minnesota. They were there to pay their respects while in Belgium, but did not have a family member there. They suggested we find the visitor's center staff member for more information.

Still on our own, we found the correct row and the gravesite for Jerome Moderski, 487th Bomber Group, who was killed on March 15, 1945, a day and a year before Allen and I were married. Denise took photos of the gravestone, which had his name, home state, and date of his death. We also did a stone rubbing of the engraving to take back to that friend's mother in Platteville.

We were about to leave when Walter Benjamin, a retired US Army soldier, approached us, offering to help us. He said he considers all visitors to be his VIPS—Very Important Persons. We told him we were not relatives but were there on behalf of friends. He excused himself and came back with American and Belgian flags and a canister that contained sand from Normandy Beach. He reached in and pulled out a handful of sand that he rubbed into the engraving on the stone to make it more visible in photographs. In the brilliant sunlight, the sand-filled letters looked like gold. He polished the rest of the gravestone with a cloth, put a flag on each side of it, clicked off several photos, and returned to the visitor's center to print them.

By the time we arrived back in the visitor's center, he had a folder of information for Jerome's family, including two large photos, and two flags to give to Marge, the mother of our friend. I repeatedly thanked him, but he said the job was a privilege for him. He was a man who served those buried there with honor and respect.

Mr. Benjamin told us that local women have adopted the cemetery, bringing flowers and visiting the gravesites. As Denise said, "I expected to feel great sadness at the cemetery. War is a horrible thing, and the fact that these young Americans died so far from their homes brings enormous grief. But after the visit to Jerome's gravesite and my conversation with Walter Benjamin, I felt a contentment and peace from the knowledge that all these years later, people still care for these young soldiers."

On this lovely Monday, the lawn was being cut with riding mowers, push mowers, and two men on their hands and knees trimming around the crosses and Stars of David with hand clippers. We were so impressed that day because we felt that the men and one woman buried there were still remembered and respected.

Losing Allen

Allen never liked to dance, something that came naturally for me coming from Europe. When his family gave us a wedding dance shortly after I arrived from Belgium, he hated it and therefore I hated it. It was a surprise, and he never liked surprises. Allen was a very reserved Norwegian, a stoic man who never liked to go out of the house for entertainment. But once we talked him into it, he could become a social butterfly.

In January 2007, he danced at his granddaughter Kelly's wedding. It was one of those dances in which all married couples start out on the dance floor and then leave as the years of their marriage were announced. With sixty-one years of marriage, we were the last on the floor. On that occasion he was happy to be dancing, and I was thrilled to be with him.

I was never an early morning person, a reason I worked the night shift at the hospital for so many years. After we were both retired, Allen was kind enough to let me sleep in despite his rising naturally at 5 a.m. daily. Allen read the paper in another room while I slept but had coffee ready for me when I got up.

On October 28, 2007, I was surprised that he let me sleep as late as I did. When I found him, Allen was half on the floor—he had suffered a devastating stroke. He died three days later on Halloween. As someone who loved the outdoors, animals, and nature, he would have hated being in a nursing home. Still, it was devastating to lose him because he was such a wonderful man, and we had such a loving marriage.

CHAPTER SEVEN

SPEAKING OUT ABOUT MY EXPERIENCES IN WORLD WAR II

I saw so many horrific things in Europe during World War II, but I did not want to burden my children with these stories. I didn't want to scare them. It was clear there was something different about me than the other mothers, but I mostly kept my life story to myself.

The first time I started talking about my experience was when my daughter, Denise, was in Girl Scouts. It was while I was a Girl Scout leader helping the girls work toward a badge that I mentioned my experiences—but without the difficult details.

Among the first speaking engagements I had was at a church in Black Hammer, Minnesota, following the 1978 broadcast of the miniseries *Holocaust*. The series was criticized by many as trivializing and commercializing the Holocaust, but it was still haunting to many people to see the images of travesties that had been done to millions of people. Knowing I was from Belgium, the pastor at that church asked me to speak about what I saw.

After that, the dam burst. I was asked to speak many places, including Norskedalen, a nature and heritage center near Coon Valley, Wisconsin, that has weekly programs on a variety of topics. I spoke each year to students at La Crescent High School in La Crescent, Minnesota, not far from my home in Houston. At La Crescent High School, Darryle Clott taught a three-month course on the Holocaust in all of her English classes. From there, I spoke with middle and elementary school students, tailoring my talk to what they would understand.

Mary answering questions after speaking to students at Longfellow Middle School in LaCrosse, Wisconsin.

After Darryle retired from La Crescent High School, she began teaching courses about the Holocaust at Viterbo University in La Crosse where I would speak. In 2005, she asked me to speak at an evening program in the Fine Arts Center.

One of the reasons it is important for people like me to tell our stories is that so many of us who witnessed the Holocaust are dying. Within a decade there will be few, if any, survivors able to tell the world what we saw. Hearing directly from someone who was there adds more credibility and meaning than a textbook description.

In one elementary school, the teacher must have explained to the students that so many people who had lived in Europe during those years were dying. After I spoke, a cute little tyke came up to me and said, "I am so happy you came to talk to us before you died." He was very sweet and very sincere.

Whenever I speak, I close my talk with words that have inspired me for decades—the quote by Martin Niemöller.[29] These words are as relevant today as they were sixty years ago:

In Germany, they came first for the communists,
and I did not speak out
because I was not a communist.

Then they came for the Jews,
and I did not speak out
because I was not a Jew.

Then they came for the trade unionists,
and I did not speak out
because I was not a trade unionist.

Then they came for the Catholics,
and I did not speak out
because I was a Protestant.

Then they came for me,
and there was no one left
to speak for me.

Niemöller, who died in 1984, was described by the US Holocaust Memorial Museum as "an ardent nationalist and prominent Protestant pastor who emerged as an outspoken public foe of Adolf Hitler and spent the last seven years of Nazi rule in concentration camps."

The museum noted the content of his quote was controversial and had been printed in different forms, referring sometimes to Catholics, Jehovah's Witnesses, Jews, Trade Unionists, Socialists, and/or Communists.

"Nonetheless his point was that Germans—in particular, he believed, the leaders of the Protestant churches—had been complicit through their silence in the Nazi imprisonment, persecution, and murder of millions of people," the museum said of him. "At the same time, however, Niemöller, like most of his compatriots, was largely silent about the persecution and mass murder of the European Jews. Only in 1963, in a West German television interview, did Niemöller acknowledge and make a statement of regret about his own anti-Semitism."[30]

I have long been inspired by his words because they speak to the need to face up to hate whenever and wherever we see it, whether it is a child who witnesses bullying or an adult who sees discrimination. If we do not, we, too, are saying by our silence that we are agreeing with the words or actions we see. And we may be the next to face hate.

An Unexpected Honor

In 1986, I received a telegram telling me that I had been chosen as a recipient of the congressionally sponsored Ellis Island Medal of Honor. I was invited to a presentation on Ellis Island on October 27, 1986, and a banquet in honor of the first recipients of this award.

I thought the telegram was a joke and almost threw it away. If not a joke, then I thought it was one of those things

A clipping from *USA Today*, 1986, announcing the first recipients of the Ellis Island Medal of Honor. Photo © USA TODAY NETWORK.

in which you pay money to have your name included in some book.

It turns out Denise had nominated me for this award, which the telegram said "honors the contributions of individuals from each of the major heritage groups that comprise the nation's population."

That first year it was awarded at a ceremony honoring the 100th anniversary of the dedication of the Statue of Liberty on October 28, 1886.

To be eligible, a candidate had to meet at least one of these standards:

- Exemplify the ideal of living a life dedicated to the American way while cherishing and preserving the values and tenets of a particular heritage group.
- Expend efforts to support, defend or highlight the values associated with American life; expend efforts to extend, preserve and expand the values associated with a particular ethnic group, or most ideally, achievements combining both.
- Contribute extraordinary service to a particular heritage group enabling the growth, preservation or revitalization of that group's participation in the diversity of American life.
- Attain special achievement in reinforcing the bonds between a heritage group and the people of its land of origin.
- Contribute distinguished service to humanity in any field, profession or occupation.

I was selected among 15,000 nominations received by the National Ethnic Coalition of Organizations, and was honored among eighty given the award its first year. This initial group included boxer Muhammad Ali, civil rights activist Rosa Parks, singer John Denver, baseball legend Joe DiMaggio, television's Walter Cronkite and Barbara Walters, former first lady Jackie Kennedy Onassis, and many others.

The selection committee said it was looking for "superstars right down to grassroots." I was the grassroots.

I may have been born in a metropolitan city, but had become a midwestern small-town woman who was giddy with excitement when talking like we were neighbors with the likes of Joe DiMaggio, Muhammad Ali, and even John Denver's mother. I remember seeing Archbishop John Cardinal O'Connor tease Barbara Walters because they were not supposed to wear the same thing—both were dressed in red. I rode with Rosa Parks in the hotel elevator. Rosa Parks! She was one of my heroes.

At the black-tie reception at the Waldorf Astoria Hotel I felt like Cinderella at the ball with all the candlelight and crystal chandeliers. Before this invitation, I didn't even know what black tie was. My only clothes were the uniforms I wore at work or my bathrobe. Denise and I shopped for a dress for that special day.

That award celebrated our country as a land of immigrants from many lands, a reason the committee wanted to honor people with a wide range of ethnicities and backgrounds. We can all trace our family history to immigration—unless we happen to be Native Americans.

That is why anti-immigrant attitudes trouble me. It is as if some Americans found it acceptable that their ancestors came here for a better life, but not "you people," whoever "you people" are.

When I was in the hospital a few years ago, I met a young pastoral care resident at Gundersen Lutheran who was from a small African country. He wanted to bring his wife and baby to the United States to be with him while he was studying here. He was turned down. I really felt for him and wondered what the reason was for denying him this opportunity to be with his family. Did the government think his wife and baby were going to blow up the country or start a revolution?

When I came to this country I experienced mixed reactions. Many people were wonderful, but there were a few family members and some neighbors who questioned Allen marrying "a girl from over there." I think some imagined I was an uncivilized waif without a brain in my head. There were moments when I was overwhelmed in those early years and could have gone back to Belgium— but not without Allen, of course.

Among the many questions that people asked me was if farmers in Europe wore wooden shoes. I explained many times that in clay-based soil, wooden shoes were worn so the soil would not stick to the shoes as they would with leather.

When I came to the United States, I didn't wear a poster announcing I was from Europe, although I'm sure my accent and limited English may have given me away as someone not from Minnesota—or Norway. I was mostly silent for decades about my experiences during World War II. I wasn't sure anyone wanted to listen.

Many displaced persons from Europe were silent—especially Holocaust survivors, who did not speak publicly about what they had endured—except with each other, for a long time. They might have been discouraged from telling their stories when they did. Perhaps people with good intentions told them to "just put it behind you and move on." That is far easier said than done in situations when you are the only survivor of your family.

If I have any message to young people, or people of any age, it is to never forget the atrocities that were carried out in Europe in the mid-twentieth century and to realize genocide can and has happened again. We must be ready to respond to injustice when we hear or witness it. Perhaps if more people had done so in the 1930s, Hitler might not have had the power to kill tens of millions of people.

Young people often tell me they could never do what I did in Europe. I tell them I was surprised myself but proud of what I did—except for the trauma I caused my family. The Germans gave us rules that made me and others rebel.

But there is something else that I hope anyone who hears or reads my story remembers as well.

Humanity in the Midst of War

Despite all the horrors—and there were many in Europe in those years—there were many acts of decency and human kindness. I learned of a kindness that occurred during the war that only became public knowledge many years later. A Belgian woman, Marie Lipstadt Pinhas, had written to a Belgian newspaper about her experience in 1945. In that letter, she described meeting a young American soldier whom she was determined to thank. Her letter, describing her experience at the end of the war, was translated into English and sent to the United States, where another veteran was determined to find the soldier who had been so kind to Marie decades earlier. Here is the letter she wrote:

> 27th April 1945. The cannons thundered the whole night and it was early in the morning that American troops liberated our concentration camp near the village of Tuerckheim, in Bavaria. No outburst surely, in enemy country, but for us, the final certitude to be free and alive.
>
> Only fourteen years old and already for me to be aware of all human cruelty—I should say inhuman cruelty, against us. A little lost, naturally—what to do with this new freedom?
>
> I walked into Tuerckheim, looking for somebody friendly, when a G.I., very tall, addressed me sharply. I didn't understand English, so I showed him my forearm on which he could clearly see my tattooed concentration camp registration number.
>
> Then, very simply, without comment, he took my hand and led me into a well-stocked clothes shop on the village place. Standing me in front of a mirror, the G.I. gave me one dress after another, one too long, the other ugly.

I was very moved with gratitude for this man, who during this terrible war, was concerned enough to want to find a nice dress for a young girl, who was wearing rags after being liberated from a concentration camp. We took a dress, without paying, while the shopkeeper looked at us in a hostile manner. The soldier was apparently very satisfied to see that I was now nicely dressed.

With a strong voice he said, "Bye-bye," leaving me and walking off into the distance. I don't remember his face, but in my mind is imprinted the memory of this soldier who gave me back the appearance of a free girl. If he is still alive—and I hope it so much—I would like him to know that I often think about him, and it would be marvelous if he could recognize himself in this story.[31]

About fifteen years after she wrote the letter in 1969, it reached the soldier, Harry Hendersin, at a reunion of the 506th Parachute Regiment of the 101st Airborne Division. Hendersin, then living in Wisconsin, placed that letter in his scrapbook and forgot about it.

In 2010 Harry was going on a Freedom Honor Flight, which honors the sacrifices of America's World War II veterans by flying them to Washington, D.C., to see the National World War II Memorial, which opened in 2004.

Phil Green, his friend who was accompanying Harry on the trip, discovered the letter in Harry's scrapbook. He talked with the Honor Flight staff, which connected Harry with personnel at Fort McCoy in Wisconsin. Harry and

Marie were connected via Skype software that allows for face-to-face calls over the Internet.

My friend Darryle Clott heard about the story and knew Denise and I planned a trip to Belgium in 2010. She gave me Marie's address in Uccle, which was not far from my family.

On the last Saturday of that visit, we met Marie and her husband and quickly felt like old friends. She and I had both gone through terrible things in those war years. We shared a commitment to tell our stories in the hope of the world not forgetting what had happened during World War II.

Marie had lost her family in Dachau, the first concentration camp created by the Nazis in 1933. Dachau, according to the US Holocaust Memorial Museum, began as a prison for political prisoners—German Communists, Social Democrats, trade unionists, and other political opponents of the Nazi regime.[32] Later Dachau held all sorts of prisoners, including tens of thousands of Jews; Roma; Jehovah's Witnesses; "asocials," who might be vagrants or nonconformists; and repeat criminal offenders. At least 188,000 prisoners were held there, and many were worked or starved to death.

American forces liberated the camp on April 26, 1945, finding more than half of the 67,775 prisoners in the camp's registry still there. Soldiers also found rail cars filled with thousands of dead bodies. About 7,000 prisoners, mostly Jews, had been forced out on a "death march" about forty-one miles south to Tegernsee in southern Germany. Those who could not keep marching were shot;

others died in route because of starvation, exhaustion, or exposure to cold.

After we shared our stories, we got up to leave Marie, thinking we had taken too much of her time. But she and her husband insisted we stay to celebrate our new friendship over champagne, chocolates, and cake. They had us take Belgian chocolates to Harry and Phil plus a small cat figurine with a sign that said, "I love you."

About a month after our return, Kim, Denise, and I drove from Houston, Minnesota, to meet Harry in Sparta, Wisconsin, where he lived in assisted living. As we walked in, we saw a smiling man sitting in the lobby awaiting us. We introduced ourselves with great excitement, entering a conference room decorated in red, white, and blue. Joining us were Harry's granddaughter, Kim; Phil, who accompanied him on the Freedom Flight; Lorrie, a Fort McCoy representative; Bill Hoel from the Honor Freedom Flight organization; and Darryle.

The coincidences and connections that brought us all together had us all shaking our heads and grinning. I bonded with Harry because we had both experienced the horrors of war and had been brought together through Marie. Harry then showed us his medals, which proved he showed great kindness and heroism on D-Day.

Harry said one of the reasons that he spent so little time with Marie was that he had to get back to his unit. The fighting was not over. But he had helped liberate Dachau and knew the horrors there. When he saw this girl and recognized she was from the camp, he wanted to do something for her.

Sadly, Harry died in August 2010, just days before a story about him was to be aired on WKBT-TV, La Crosse. We felt fortunate to have helped make this connection between two heroes sixty-five years after they first met.

His story was just one example of the humanity that managed to shine through in a time of great despair. Another is an anonymous quote written on the wall of a German cellar where Jews hid from the Nazis during World War II:

> *I believe in the sun when it does not shine. I believe*
> *in love even when I do not feel it. I believe in God*
> *even when he is silent.*

Whoever wrote these words kept his or her humanity in a time when it was lacking in the world. It tells us that while we cannot prevent inhumanity in others, we can and must preserve our own.

Mary Rostad at the 2011 Teaching the Holocaust Workshop at Viterbo University, LaCrosse, Wisconsin.

EPILOGUE

BY SUSAN T. HESSEL

There is no way to express the sorrow of Mary dying in the midst of this book's production. She'd had a chance to review a first draft, but sadly, developed pancreatic cancer that took her from all of us way too soon. It only made the need to get this book into print more urgent. And so we are, despite the irony of the title, *Squirrel Is Alive*.

As the Rev. Lane Zaffke, who officiated at her funeral said, "You did not have to talk to Mary long to get a sense of her humbleness. When I asked her about her work in the Resistance, she merely shrugged her shoulders, as she often did throughout her life. She merely shrugged her shoulders and said, 'This is what I can do.'

"A lot of us when we look at the world and hear the news think the world is overwhelming. The problems that we face are overwhelming and we think, 'What can I do?'" he continued. "Too often we give up or we think what we do doesn't matter. Mary would shrug her shoulders and say, 'I will do what I can.' She would think, 'I cannot give up.' When she was faced with Nazis, she merely shrugged her shoulders and joined the Resistance. She knew evil when she saw it, and she knew whatever little bit she could do would add up or it would be joined with other people who would add another little bit and eventually they would change the world."

I first met Mary some years ago when I heard her speak about her experience fighting back against the Nazis in Belgium and later in France. She showed a spunk and courage that most of us need to have—but few do. When I happened to walk into her room shortly after her cancer diagnosis, I told her about the spunk I saw in her.

"I'm going to need spunk now," she told me.

She had every intention of fighting back against the cancer, but pancreatic is an adversary every bit as nasty as the Nazis. Still, she asked me what chemotherapy was like—I had it two years ago when I was fifty-seven, thirty years younger than she would have been. Yes, Mary was a fighter. She wanted to fight cancer the way she fought any other wrong in life.

I did not know Mary as well as many others, but I had heard her speak several times. About the third time, I wanted to help her write her story. She told me she'd think about it when she felt better.

It took a good two years to convince her to give me that privilege. She resisted for several reasons, including the belief that what she did was not so important—that shoulder shrugging that her pastor mentioned. She also wanted to wait until she felt stronger, although most people only saw strength in her.

I think those of us who heard her speak were impressed because she really was a tiny-figured girl and then woman, a David fighting against Goliath.

Growing up Jewish in a post–World War II neighborhood in suburban St. Louis, I always hid from the Holocaust. My family had all immigrated to the United States at the turn into the twentieth century, which means no one had died at the hands of the Nazis. Still, having people hate me because of my religion was very personal. I know my family would have been killed had we lived there.

Having just helped an Auschwitz survivor tell her story, I had finally opened up to the horror that was the Nazis in World War II. Mary's story was important to tell because even though she was not a targeted minority, she fought back against evil when she saw it. She was a role model for how we should all speak out against evil. We all need an infusion of her tremendous courage.

Thankfully, Darryle Clott, her good friend and a Holocaust educator, was determined to get Mary's story preserved and shared. Mary just kept shrugging her shoulders.

But Mary didn't realize how much she inspired people. She reminded us of what we could be and should be, which is a message particularly important to young people whom she spoke to in schools.

Mary kept so silent about all this for the first thirty to forty years she was in the United States. With her accent, she felt like an other—someone different from the people she met and lived with in Houston, Minnesota. Like Holocaust survivors who did not speak out for decades, she felt no one wanted to hear her story. Most people who had experienced Europe in those years just wanted to get on with their lives.

Once she became a mother, Mary was a bit embarrassed about her activities because she realized the impact of what she did on her parents. They had no idea where she was for two years in a time when people disappeared, never to be seen again.

Once the Nazis arrived in the city she loved, Mary put herself—and her family—at risk every single day. That is the real reason that she left. If arrested by the Nazis while doing resistance work, she would have been punished severely—and likely killed—along with her entire family. Still, she looked back at that decision with embarrassment, believing she had been cruel to her family.

Learning of her death, I wish I had one more interview with Mary, although after that I would have wanted another and another. Others would have wanted another cup of coffee, another quilt, another salad, another holiday spent with her and then another and another.

As the Rev. Zaffke said, "Mary would have merely shrugged her shoulders and said, 'It is not much.' It isn't much but it was more valuable than gold, her love and her care. It was living out the ministry that God had given her: not giving up, not being overwhelmed, not being frozen in the clutch of anxiety."

Instead her gift was to "show God's love and goodness and God's justice and God's peace," the pastor said. It is our hope that through *Squirrel Is Alive* our special Mary truly lives on.

AFTERWORD

BY DARRYLE CLOTT

You just read an amazing story about a true heroine, and I am quite certain you fell in love with Mary. She had that effect on people. I had the honor of knowing Mary both professionally, as a person involved in my work in Holocaust education, but also as my dear friend who became like a mother figure to me. I want to tell you about my beloved friend and colleague who was a remarkable woman in all stages of her life.

When Mary's daughter, Denise, was young, she was hospitalized having her tonsils removed. Mary stayed with her in the hospital, helping care for her. The nurses at Gundersen Lutheran Medical Center in La Crosse were so impressed they suggested Mary work at the hospital. The next week she was working as a nursing assistant and stayed there for thirty years and eventually became a licensed practical nurse. She had the opportunity to become a registered nurse, but declined as she wanted to do bedside nursing, not paperwork, as she thought many RNs seemed to be doing. After thirty years full time, she worked another ten years, including being on call twenty-four hours a day in the role of taking corneas for transplant for the Wisconsin Eye Bank until her own failing eyesight made that impossible.

Mary's special love was for the neuro patient, especially the very ill ones, admitted with severe head injury or a spinal cord injury after some type of trauma. These types of patients needed above all a nurse with neuro knowledge and experience and excellent, consistent nursing care for their best outcomes. Mary was sharp with great assessment skills, and not much would get by her. She could catch subtle changes in a patient's condition quickly and get them the help they needed. Mary worked her marathon of ten 8-hour shifts all in a row, which then gave her four days off to recuperate, catch up on her sleep, and spend time with her family. This kept her with the same patient assignments, and she was able to give them consistent, wonderful care.

Several nurses told me it would be hard to adequately show the impact Mary had on so many young nurses. One was a brand-new graduate nurse who was nervous and unsure as she entered her first job and was assigned to Mary's unit that specialized in the care of patients with neuroscience disorders. She had limited experience in this very specialized medical field. Luckily for her, Mary took her under her wing. After Mary heard her concerns, she put her arm around her, gave her a huge hug, and told her she would make a wonderful neuro nurse and that experience would provide her with confidence.

Mary became her mentor whom she trusted to provide her with guidance, and she showed her the techniques necessary to care for a patient population she grew to love. Mary never made her feel inadequate, and taught her in a positive way, always giving her the chance to feel confident in her own skills. She told of the love Mary's patients had for her, and how nurses would trade shifts just to work with her. Mary continued to help her throughout her career and now, fifty years later, as a retired RN, she still remembers Mary who made the world a better place through her compassion for her patients, her humor, and her true love of nursing.

At work, Mary was famous for her salads. No matter what was happening on the floor, when they knew there was a "Mary Salad" waiting for them at the desk, they could make it. When they saw her walking in with that huge salad bowl wrapped in a dish towel with the four corners tied together—sometimes the bowl was so big she had to bring it in on a wheelchair—they knew everything would be OK. On those nights, the night pharmacist, respiratory therapists, residents, orderlies, doctors, security, and lab people would also just happen to wander by. The staff knew to have extra plates and forks.

Also, back in the day, Mary found a way to access the kitchen during the wee hours and mothered many a hungry resident with a homemade omelet.

Sometimes they would run short of necessary laundry items during the night shift. Mary was very resourceful—when the powers that be found her hidden cupboards where she would store up supplies, she moved her stash to the ceiling tiles. Through the years many a construction worker probably scratched his head wondering about towels and washcloths above the ceiling tiles.

Mary baked rum balls for a New Year's Eve she was working. A young orderly, who later became a doctor, tried one and liked it so much he continued to have one after another, not realizing they contained alcohol. Later, the nurses found him snoozing on the desk.

The hospital gang felt blessed beyond words to have had Mary as their coworker and friend. She was their mother. She fed them, she listened to them, and she taught them. They cried together and laughed often.

For many years Mary was a Girl Scout leader with her scouts meeting in Mary's home after school. Quite often, Mary had worked an overnight shift at the hospital, and her scouts would be standing on her doorstep, knocking until they woke her up from her much-needed sleep. Mary's adorable dog, Choux-choux, would help by barking their arrival to Mary as well. Mary would eventually, bleary-eyed, open the door and welcome them in.

They loved listening to her talk to them with her French accent. Anything non-Scandinavian seemed practically exotic. As the meeting progressed, she would become fully awake and excited to be with them again as they made their sit-upons, worked on various merit badges, or planned for their next parade appearance. They would ask about her family back in Belgium. Letters were the mode of communication then, and it was hard for the scouts to imagine leaving all they knew and starting life in a new land so far away from family. Mary would tell them that she could not imagine a life without her Allen. To young Girl Scouts, it was the stuff romance novels were written about.

Mary was the ear-piercing queen of Minnesota. She pierced the ears of most of the Houston girls during the sixties. In those "pre-mall" days, Mary was the only trusted provider of that service in Houston.

Mary was a wonderful quilter, and many of us are fortunate to have her lovely creations. Her son Kim coached the Aquinas girls' basketball team, and Mary always made quilted bags for every one of his seniors for graduation.

Mary was a member of three quilting groups. She was the contact for the Ronald McDonald House quilts. One of her favorite things was helping make, collect, and deliver hundreds to the Rochester Minnesota House for the children. She also helped make Quilts of Valor for wounded warriors or returning veterans and quilts that were sent overseas.

As her vision began to fail, she continued to quilt by feel, and instead of making large quilts, she made small projects such as lap quilts, wall hangings, bags, and table runners—and once a jacket that ended up as a toaster cover.

Mary was a great cook. I never entered her comfortable home without being treated to her splendid homemade desserts. Sometimes I took reporters and cameramen out to Mary's home for stories. They would always be happily surprised when we would sit at her dining room table beautifully set with her good china to have coffee and homemade dessert. Evidently this is not the norm when they go out on stories.

Mary gave me a copy of the *Cross of Christ Church Cookbook*. I was a little surprised when I read it and found her name on only one recipe, so I asked her about it. She then went through the cookbook and showed me the many recipes she had given to others—with their names on them. At that point I renamed the cookbook *Mary & the Cross of Christ Church Cookbook*.

Mary's family was the most important thing in her life. Next to family, her many loyal friends were her greatest treasures, but Mary was also a gift to educators. She was the ultimate teacher's teacher. For years she shared her story in classrooms throughout western Wisconsin and southeastern Minnesota.

She spoke to all my English classes at La Crescent High School in La Crescent, Minnesota, from 1998 when I began teaching the Holocaust until I retired in 2004. After that she shared her story with classes at Viterbo University in La Crosse, Wisconsin, where I taught History of the Holocaust, along with speaking to my Learning in Retirement Classes at University of Wisconsin–La Crosse, the Midwest Holocaust Education Consortium, and to the Holocaust Educators' Workshops at Viterbo.

I saw her mesmerize students from the ages of fifteen to eighty, and times too numerous to count, handle an auditorium of 150 high school freshmen where, because students were so engaged with Mary and her message, one could hear a pin drop. On November 8, 2005, she dazzled an audience of 1,150 people who filled the Viterbo Fine Arts Center to hear Mary speak as part of our Perspectives on the Holocaust Series. I can still see her that night dressed in her purple dress, moving slowly up the stairs to the stage on her son Kim's arm, cane in her other hand. She sat down, put her hands in her lap, looked up at the crowd and without a note, spoke for forty-five minutes. Before she spoke, I would always tell the audience, "Prepare to fall in love," and they always did.

I believe I heard Mary give her captivating message at least fifty times, and every time I heard her, I learned something new about what it was like to live under occupation and her work as a teenager in the resistance against the Nazis during the Holocaust. Mary did not think she was a hero, but I know she was. She was a hero to every person privileged to hear her story.

Through hearing her remarkable experiences, people were able to sense the hunger, the fear, and more than anything, the loneliness Mary felt those two years walking across Belgium and France. She worked in the Belgian resistance and French underground delivering secret messages, small arms, and sometimes ammunition to undercover agents and freedom fighters. She covered what territory she could by day, sleeping, if lucky in churches or railroad sidecars, and if unlucky in barns, for she was deathly afraid of mice. She ate carrots and apples she found along the road or a rare piece of bread, which she considered a feast—if she was fortunate enough to find a family willing to give her that treat.

Can any of us possibly imagine what it must have been like to be a young woman, seventeen years old, shutting the door that spring morning when she left her home in Brussels, Belgium, with only the clothes on her back, not knowing when she would return home to the safety of her family?

Adventure and heroics aside, I am a hopeless romantic and am drawn to the part of the story when Mary meets her American soldier, Allen, with whom she fell in love and married, which brought her to Houston,

Minnesota, and to us here in the Coulee Region seventy-six years ago. (She arrived in Spring Grove, Minnesota, May 19, 1946.)

I am honored to be able to share a love letter written by Allen to Mary while they were separated.

25 October 1945 Germany

My Mary darling

I have written one letter tonight but now as I was going to bed I was seeing your most beautiful face again and right now I am hearing "Stardust" from the next house. So you must know how I feel and what I am thinking. Darling what is it that makes me love you so? Tell me dearest what is it? You know Mary as I am sitting here writing I can see your face just like you are when you smile, and you seem so real, as if I could reach out and touch you. Please don't laugh at me for saying that because it all seems so real as if nobody but you are here with me. But that is the way it should be is it not darling? You're the only one that should be in my mind and in my heart. I was looking at your picture a little while ago and please don't laugh at this but I almost cried. It's just that without you life doesn't mean a thing to me. That's true darling. I don't care what happens I'm coming back it just can't be any other way for me. Darling now I am going to bed and dream about you. I'll meet you in a dream tonight. Goodnight my darling little wife. This I say with all my heart. Here are a million kisses. [I questioned Mary's daughter, Denise, about Allen's use of "wife" here, since the letter is dated October 25, 1945, and they did not get married until March 16, 1946. She said she thought her dad was using it as a term of endearment.]

> From your husband
> Love you darling

In 1986 Mary received the Ellis Island Medal of Honor Award, the first year it was given, for her work in the resistance. The medal is presented on the island by the National Ethnic Coalition to "American citizens of diverse origins for their outstanding contributions to their communities, their nation, and the world." Selected from among 15,000 nominations, Mary was one of eighty winners, including Muhammad Ali, Rosa Parks, Joe DiMaggio, Walter Cronkite, Barbara Walters, and Jackie Kennedy Onassis.

She would tell about being at the reception at the Waldorf Astoria Hotel in New York City, feeling like Cinderella at the ball with all the candlelight and crystal chandeliers and not knowing what "black tie" even meant. She said that her only clothes were her work uniforms and her bathrobe. Denise took her shopping for a dress for that special day. She always kidded about the selection committee saying they were looking for "superstars right down to the grassroots" and would say, "Clearly I was the grassroots."

One day at her home I asked her if I could see her medal. She could not find it and went searching, finally finding it stuffed in the back of a drawer. From then on, she had it displayed, knowing I would ask to see it each time I came visiting.

When Mary was honored at Congregation Sons of Abraham Synagogue in La Crosse, Wisconsin, in May 2011, Rabbi Simcha Prombaum asked me to tell the audience what I learned from Mary, and I told them, and now I tell you that from Mary I learned humility and humor and class, but most of all, love.

I would like to conclude by sharing a poem written by Dana Humphrey from St. Louis, Missouri, after she heard Mary speak at our Midwest Holocaust Educators' Consortium. Incidentally "Squirrel," part of the title, was Mary's nickname as a child in Girl Scouts and her code name in the resistance as it was too dangerous to use real names.

Lessons From Night School: How to Be a Squirrel
In Honor of Mary Rostad
By Dana Humphrey

Turn street signs around to confuse the Nazis
Take a gun butt in the head for refusing
to get off the sidewalk
Steal your mother's sugar ration and
put it in Nazi gas tanks
Trade silver and gold uniform buttons
sliced off with razor blades

File down the switches of Nazi flashlights
so they are useless
Sleep in church pews, barns and empty rail cars
Fake a toothache with tears
Learn how to live alone without friends
Remain silent for thirty years
Receive the Ellis Island Medal of Honor
Share the story of resistance
Become a Hero

Mary was my teacher and treasure, but most of all, my dear friend.

Elie Wiesel with Mary Rostad and Darryle Clott at a donor reception in the Reinhart Center at Viterbo University, La Crosse, Wisconsin, on September 27, 2006. Photo taken by David Joseph Marcou of La Crosse, who was Viterbo's official Elie Wiesel photographer that day.

NOTES

1. Alan Bullock, *Hitler: A Study in Tyranny*, abridged ed. (New York: Harper & Row, 1971), p. 202.
2. "Treaty of Versailles," 1919, US Holocaust Memorial Museum, http://www.ushmm.org/wlc/en/article.php?ModuleId= 10005425.
3. "Making a Leader," US Holocaust Memorial Museum, http://www.ushmm.org/wlc/en/article.php?ModuleId=10007817.
4. Roger Motz, *Belgium Unvanquished* (London: Lindsay Drummond, 1943), p. 2.
5. Ibid., p. 3.
6. Ibid.
7. "Walloons," http://www.everyculture.com/wc/Afghanistan-to-Bosnia-Herzegovina/Walloons.html#ixzz18g6imbAU.
8. Bernard A. Cook, *Belgium: A History* (New York: Peter Lang Publishing, 2002), p. 113.
9. Motz, *Belgium Unvanquished*, p. 5.
10. Ibid., p. 10.
11. "Resistance during the Holocaust," US Holocaust Memorial Museum, https://www.ushmm.org/m/pdfs/20000831-resistance-bklt.pdf.
12. Motz, *Belgium Unvanquished*, p. 86.
13. Alden Oreck and Mitchell Bard, "Belgium Virtual Jewish History Tour," http://www.jewishvirtuallibrary.org/jsource/vjw/Belgium.html.
14. "Breendonk Memorial," http://www.breendonk.be/EN/index.html (accessed 2011).
15. "Breedonk (Belgium)," http://www.jewishgen.org/Forgotten-Camps/Camps/BreendEng.html.
16. "Andre de Jongh: Organiser of the Comet Line," http://www.independent.co.uk/news/obituaries/andre-de-jongh-organiser-of-the-comet-line-763264.html.
17. "The Comete Escape Line," https://ww2escapelines.co.uk/belgium-france/comete/.
18. "Andre de Jongh."

19. Edward Stourton, "Pyrenees Hikers Remember WWII Escapees," BBC News, http://www.bbc.co.uk/news/world-europe-15690262.

20. Ibid.

21. "'Agent Garbo,' the Spy Who Lied About D-Day," https://www. npr.org/2012/07/07/156189716/agent-garbo-the-spy-who-lied-about-d-day.

22. "What Does the D in D-Day Mean?" http://www.army.mil/d-day/.

23. "Eisenhower's Speech to Troops on D-Day (June 6, 1944)," https://www.jewishvirtuallibrary.org/eisenhower-s-speech-to-troops-on-d-day.

24. "'C-Rats' Fueled Troops During and After World War II," https:// www.defense.gov/News/Feature-Stories/story/Article/1933268/ c-rats-fueled-troops-during-and-after-world-war-ii/.

25. Letter from Frank William Clarke to his sister Vera, Thursday, 7th September 1944. Maggie O'Neill of the "Action Desk–Sheffield" Team posted this letter on behalf of Kathleen Clarke to WW2 People's War online archive of wartime memories contributed by members of the public and gathered by the BBC. The archive can be found at https://www.bbc.co.uk/history/ ww2peopleswar/stories/79/a4801079.shtml.

26. Dwight D. Eisenhower, *Crusade in Europe* (New York: Doubleday, 1948), p. 296.

27. "Holocaust Denial: Frau Ilse Koch and General Lucius Clay," http://www.jewishvirtuallibrary.org/jsource/Holocaust/skin. html.

28. "Battle of the Bulge: The German Counteroffensive," http:// worldwar2history.info/Bulge/.

29. Martin Niemöller, US Memorial Holocaust Museum, http:// www.ushmm.org/wlc/en/article.php?ModuleId=10007392 (accessed 2011).

30. Ibid.

31. "A Soldier and the Dress," WKBT Television, La Crosse, WI, August 25–26, 2010.

32. "Dachau," US Holocaust Memorial Museum, http://www. ushmm.org/wlc/en/article.php?ModuleId=10005214.

DISCUSSION QUESTIONS FOR *SQUIRREL IS ALIVE*

1. Have there been occasions in your life when you wish you took action to defend a person or an idea, but didn't? What kept you from doing so?

2. Why did Mary feel she had to fight back against the Nazis? How effective do you think she was? Can you give examples to support your opinion?

3. Do you think Mary should have left her parents' home? How dangerous do you think it was? How dangerous would it have been if she had stayed? Look for examples in the book to support your opinions.

4. What were Mary's greatest challenges on her journey? Why do you think they were so difficult?

5. Can you imagine yourself on the road for months and even years during a conflict like World War II? What would you find to be the most difficult part? From your reading, what can you infer about what was most difficult for Mary?

6. What was the value of friendship in Mary's life? What was the value of family? Is it important to have support from friends and family in order to make difficult choices? Why or why not?

7. Do you think you would stand up in the face of injustice? Have you done so? If yes, what was it like? If not, why?

8. Should society expect teenagers to take action when they see injustices in the world? Why or why not?

9. Is there anything you will do differently in your life because of reading this book?

10. How would you want people to remember you?

CONTRIBUTORS

Susan T. Hessel was a personal historian dedicated to preserving life stories of individuals. A board member of the Association of Personal Historians, she was especially honored to work with those who have stood up in the face of repression and adversity, and through her writing, she was able to bring untold stories of human heroism to light. She saw all humans as equal and equally deserving of care and compassion, of having their stories told. Susan's indomitable spirit enabled her to dig deep into the lives and passions of everyday heroes, preserving the stories of individuals, families, organizations, businesses, and communities. Her skill in crafting narratives that drew people into her stories was unrivaled.

In 2011, Susan agreed to help write Mary Rostad's story, the Belgian teenager who worked for the Belgian resistance and French underground at great personal peril. The result is the book you have just read—a story of incredible bravery and courage that Susan with great determination wove into a book that is ultimately compelling, sobering, and triumphant. By helping bring Mary's personal account to light, Susan provided an invaluable service to Holocaust educators and students around the globe, as well as anyone wanting to learn more about the Holocaust.

 **Stephen Feinberg** had the honor of working at the United States Holocaust Memorial Museum (USHMM) in Washington, D.C., from 1996 to 2011. From 1996 to 2000, he was responsible for the development and implementation of the Museum Teacher Fellowship Program. As director of the National Outreach program at the USHMM from 2000 to 2009, he was responsible for the creation, design, and implementation of the museum's entire national educational outreach program. He was the special assistant for Education Programs in the National Institute for Holocaust Education (NIHE) at the USHMM from 2009 to 2011. In this capacity, he coordinated NIHE's International Educational activities as well as directing the USHMM's teacher education programs in California, Florida, Texas, and Illinois.

He was a member of the United States delegation to the International Holocaust Remembrance Alliance (IHRA)

from 1999 to 2011, working extensively with the IHRA Education Working Group. In addition to conducting teacher training programs across the United States, he has also coordinated or participated in programs in Europe, South America, Africa, Asia, Australia, and New Zealand.

He joined the USHMM's staff in Washington in 1996, but had been an educational consultant for the museum since 1990. He is the coeditor, with Dr. Samuel Totten, of *Essentials of Holocaust Education* (Routledge, 2016) and *Teaching and Studying The Holocaust* (Allyn & Bacon, 2000).

Prior to his work at the museum, he was a social studies teacher in public and private schools in Massachusetts, Pennsylvania, and Paris, France. He also served as a Peace Corps volunteer in Morocco (1968–1970) and Thailand (1974–1975). Mr. Feinberg received his bachelor's degree in history from UCLA and his master's degree from Harvard University's Graduate School of Education.

Darryle Clott earned a bachelor's degree in 1966 and a master's in 1971 from The University of Wisconsin–La Crosse. She retired from La Crescent (Minnesota) High School in 2004 where she taught a comprehensive unit on the Holocaust for several years in her English classes. The classes inspired her to attend the Teachers' Summer Institute on Holocaust and Jewish Studies and Jewish Resistance in Poland and Israel in 2001, and she is currently on their Alumni Advisory Board. As her interest in the Holocaust grew, Clott became a member of the American Friends of the Jewish Fighters Museum Consortium of Holocaust Educators and is the founder of the Midwest Holocaust Education Consortium. She is a Teacher Fellow at the United States Holocaust Memorial Museum in Washington, D.C.

Darryle leads Holocaust Educator Workshops and is an associate of the Ethics in Leadership Institute at Viterbo University. She is a member of the Chancellor's Community Council at the University of Wisconsin–La Crosse. She is instrumental in bringing Holocaust survivors to the La Crosse community at Viterbo University, including Nobel Peace Prize winner Elie Wiesel, Presidential Medal of Honor winner Gerda Weissmann Klein, and Otto Frank's stepdaughter, Eva Schloss.

Darryle was a participant in the 2006 Educators' Seminar of the Educational Program on Yiddish Culture at the YIVO Institute for Jewish Research in New York City. She is on the Editorial Board of Yeshiva University's *PRISM: An Interdisciplinary Journal for Holocaust Educators*. Darryle was honored with the Gregory P. Wegner Holocaust Education Award at the Congregation Sons of Abraham Synagogue in 2008 and 2014 and is the Graff Distinguished Alumnus Award winner for 2008 at the University of Wisconsin–La Crosse. In 2009, Darryle was chosen to be part of a League of Women Voters project,

"The Road She Traveled," for local women who have had a significant impact on their community.

Darryle is the 2009 La Crosse Toastmasters' Communication and Leadership award winner. In October 2010, she was one of ten American Holocaust educators chosen to travel to Poland to study Holocaust pedagogy with Polish Holocaust educators in a program sponsored by the Polish Embassy in Washington, D.C. The La Crosse area YWCA Tribute to Outstanding Women Trailblazer Award was presented to Darryle in November 2010. In May 2011, Darryle was given the Ellis Island Medal of Honor. The medals are presented on Ellis Island to American citizens of diverse origins for their outstanding contributions to their communities, their nation, and the world.

In April 2014, Darryle was honored by Fort McCoy with the Patriotic Civilian Service Award in appreciation for exceptional support to the Fort McCoy community of soldiers and civilians.

Darryle received the Pope John XXIII Award for Distinguished Service from Viterbo University in May 2017. The award, the highest nonacademic award conferred by Viterbo, is given to those who have distinguished themselves through outstanding leadership and through service to higher education, to community, and to humankind.

In January 2018, Darryle received the Iverson Freking Ecumenical Recognition Award, which recognizes the dedication of people to ecumenical endeavors and who reflect a positive commitment to Coulee Region communities. Darryle is the 2019 Mrs. Oktoberfest.